Down *in the* Valley

Our Acquaintance with Grief

Frank Hawkins

© 2017
Published in the United States by Nurturing Faith Inc., Macon GA,
www.nurturingfaith.net.

Library of Congress Cataloging-in-Publication Data is available.

ISBN 978-1-63528-010-4

All rights reserved. Printed in the United States of America

Unless noted otherwise, Scripture citations are taken from
the Revised Standard Version (RSV).

*In some illustrations / stories, names have been changed to protect
the privacy of individuals concerned.*

Interior and cover design by Amy C. Cook

CONTENTS

Acknowledgments v
Prologue: Pastoral Insights About Grief vii
Introduction: Down in the Valley 1

PART ONE: Horizontal Grief 5
Grief and Life Stages 9
Grieving for Sabbath Rest 23
The Power of Hope 27

PART TWO: Categories of Grief 35
Anticipatory Grief 39
Delayed Grief 43
Prolonged Grief 47
Distorted Grief 49
Pathological Grief 51

PART THREE: Vertical Grief 53
Grief and the Image of God 57
Biblical Examples of Vertical Grief 67

Epilogue: The Various Faces of Tears 75

DEDICATION

To my wife, Pat, with whom I have shared life, love, and learning for 60 years, and who was loved and affirmed in all of the churches we served for the person she was and continues to be.

This book is published through a
gift from Jack C. Jr. and Eve Bishop
in honor of Frank Hawkins.

ACKNOWLEDGMENTS

I want to thank the church families that have blessed my family through the years:

- Northside Baptist Church, Rock Hill, South Carolina
- Harmony Baptist Church, Edgemoor, South Carolina
- Old Fort Baptist Church, Old Fort, South Carolina
- Melbourne Heights Baptist Church, Louisville, Kentucky
- First Baptist Church, Statesboro, Georgia
- First Baptist Church, Kingsport, Tennessee
- First Baptist Church, Black Mountain, North Carolina
- First Baptist Church, Whiteville, North Carolina
- First Baptist Church, Wallace, North Carolina
- First Baptist Church, Wilmington, North Carolina

In all of these churches we were accepted as fellow Christians seeking to grow, serve, and become more mature persons. Thank you for loving us and allowing us to love you in our valley and victory experiences.

I want to thank my friend, Kenan Maready, for his excellent technical assistance and expertise in getting this book in presentable form. Kenan is a fellow author and has self-published three books:

Chinquapin—The Way We Lived
Chinquapin—All It's Cracked Up To Be
New Hanover High School—Class of '54

Finally, I want to thank my son, Todd, for his invaluable guidance in preparing the manuscript for publishing review and Jackie Riley, managing editor for Nurturing Faith, for her outstanding care and competent leadership in preparing my book for publication.

"Any man's death diminishes me, because I am involved in mankind."
—*John Donne*

PROLOGUE

Pastoral Insights About Grief

As I began my 14th year as senior pastor of the First Baptist Church in Kingsport, Tennessee, I felt the need of a break for rest—for mental and spiritual replenishment. I learned of Duke University Divinity School's Fellows Program, basically for United Methodist ministers, to address needs such as mine. To my surprise, when I wrote a letter asking if the program might have room for a weary Baptist pastor, I received a positive response. Not only was I accepted, but I also received a scholarship to help pay for lodging, meals, books, and other expenses. I was delighted!

I began the program, designed for three consecutive Februarys, in 1993. Participants shared in group meetings once a week for fellowship, book reviews, and dialogue (led by mentor pastors and faculty professors). Each minister had a carrel in the divinity school library for research on ministry themes relevant to parish and church field life. Beyond those basic expectations, we were free to audit classes, attend worship services, have informal colleague discussions (usually at meal times), and dream about a chance to see the Duke Blue Devils play basketball in Cameron Indoor Stadium—a feat I achieved twice during my February days at Duke University.

I chose grief as the theme of my ministry research. Although I already had 33 years of pastoral experience, I wanted to learn more about the nature of grief. I wanted to be a better minister during people's experiences of loss and sorrow.

My decision to dig deeper into "the dynamics of grief" (the title given to an outstanding book about grief written by Dr. David Switzer) came in part as the result of a dream I had in 1977 when I was pastor of the First Baptist Church in Statesboro, Georgia. In the dream I was standing before a beautiful multicolored stained glass window with Marion Cornwell and James Kirkpatrick, two people I knew well.

Marion was a member of Harmony Baptist Church in Edgemoor, South Carolina, my first pastorate after graduating in 1960 from Southeastern Baptist Theological Seminary in Wake Forest, North Carolina. In my first visits in church members' homes where there had been suffering and loss, I heard repeatedly about Mrs. Cornwell. When I visited Marion in her home I learned why.

She had lost her husband, C. C. Cornwell, to a massive heart attack right at the peak of a very successful career in the farming business. One day, all alone at home, months into her grief, she said she was reading a small book about suffering in which the author wrote these words, "We need to be good stewards of our sufferings." Mrs. Cornwell said she put the book down and said to herself, "That's what I'm going to do: be a good steward of my grief." And she did! Our church field became her parish. Where there were hurts and loss, Marion Cornwell showed up with compassion and practical care. How fortunate I was as a first-time, young pastor in a small country, antebellum church to have an associate pastor as a colleague in ministry!

James (Jim) Kirkpatrick, his wife Bonnie, and their four children (two each from previous marriages) were active at Melbourne Heights Baptist Church in Louisville, Kentucky, when I became their pastor in 1971. One of my first home visits was to the Kirkpatrick family. After talking with two of the children about the meaning of Christian baptism, I turned to Jim, who was listening with focused attention, and said, "Jim, two of your children are ready to be baptized. How wonderful it would be for you to lead them as their father in being baptized as new Christians." (I knew Jim had never been baptized). He immediately responded, "I'm ready!"

Jim and Bonnie Kirkpatrick and Marion Cornwell had all experienced significant grief. Jim and Bonnie had lived through painful divorces, but had chosen to live again in new relationships as marital partners and parents. Their previous spouses were still alive, and they had grieved the loss of those once-vital connections. Marion's loss was different. Her spouse was dead, but she was not. Her challenge was to come out of her acquaintance with grief and to live again. She did! So did Jim and Bonnie.

I still cherish the memories of my two Februarys spent at Duke Divinity School. I was unable to take part in the Fellows Program a third year due to another opportunity: I was elected president of the Tennessee Baptist Convention in 1995, and knew the demands of that challenge would render a month away from Tennessee not fair to either opportunity. My experience at Duke in the mid 1990s, however, was a double blessing.

First, the time away from the daily responsibilities of pastoral ministry interrupted a process all too common for ministers: burn down toward burnout. Second, what I learned about the universal experience of grief—coupled with more than three decades of walking with people through their valley times—has given me a deeper appreciation for the role of ministers and, hopefully, a keener insight into the role of grief in the never-ending changes we experience as relational beings. Following are some of those insights:

• Grief is a gift inherent in all persons. It is not a weakness, but a natural response of persons to actual or perceived losses of needed and cherished relationships. The relationships can be personal or interpersonal or to objects or things.

• Grief is not a choice. It is a response to separation caused by death, accident, or choice.

- People grieve differently according to their temperament and personality. Some grieve openly and publicly. Others grieve inwardly and privately. Most people are both private and public in their grief expressions. The important thing is to own and express our grief so that grief does not own us.

- Grief should not come to stay. When it does, it becomes an unhealthy dwelling place instead of a transition toward the renewal of life. Some people, however, take longer to process their grief than others. In our busy world we cannot schedule grief as a hurried event in the fast lane.

- Grief can be resolved in two ways. It can end with (1) acceptance of the loss, which is usually presented as the last stage in the grief process, or (2) with reconciliation of the persons who have experienced the pain of separation. The basic theme of the Bible deals with God's grief that refuses to accept the loss of his creation. God has on his mind and heart a reunion with what he has lost, not the acceptance of the loss. This can be true when married couples are separated. They have a choice to make: they can divorce or reconcile. There are times when divorce may be the better choice.

- There are two dimensions or directions to grief. (1) Transcendent or vertical grief looks up and says there is someone above us with whom we are related and attached and from whom we can be separated. When separation occurs, it produces grief in the transcendent one and in those created by and related to the transcendent reality or person. This helps to explain the universal presence of religion in all civilizations, past and present. The word "religion" means to reconnect what was once connected and has become separated. (2) Horizontal grief emerges between imperfect human beings. It is both interpersonal and intrapersonal.

- Pastors and counselors relate to people who experience all of the above-mentioned dimensions of grief. To relate and minister well, they must know and care for their members and counselees as they are—not as they may idealize them to be.

- In the Bible and in life, guilt is inseparably related to grief. When guilt is separated from grief, the Good News may become bad news and sustain unresolved grief and shallow, dysfunctional spirituality. The parable of the prodigal son illustrates well this dynamic connection between grief and guilt.

- Grief and joy co-exist in the same persons. They tend to enrich life when experienced as opposites that are paradoxically related as friends and not enemies. For example, Jesus was a man of sorrow. However, as he experienced the grief of his impending death, he spoke to his disciples about his own joy and about his desire that their joy might be full also (John 15:11).

- In order to relate more effectively to those who are experiencing grief, ministers and counselors must be in touch with their own history of grief and open to being comforted.

These aspects of grief will guide and permeate what I write in this book. For a fuller presentation about the many aspects of grief, I recommend the following books:

Kubler-Ross, Elizabeth. *On Death and Dying*. New York: Macmillan Company, 1969.
Oates, Wayne E. *Anxiety in Christian Experience*. Philadelphia: Westminster Press, 1955.
Switzer, David K. *The Dynamics of Grief*. Nashville: Abingdon Press, 1970.
Westberg, Granger. *Good Grief*. Philadelphia: Fortress Press, 1962.

INTRODUCTION

Down in the Valley

In the summer of 2016 I had a vivid dream. In it Pat and I were still living in Kingsport, Tennessee, and Wayne E. Oates was a guest in our home. A little background: Dr. Oates served as senior professor of psychology of religion at Southern Baptist Theological Seminary in Louisville, Kentucky, and as professor of psychiatry and behavioral sciences at the University of Louisville School of Medicine during the 1960s and 70s. I am one of a multitude of pastors and ministers who have been blessed by Dr. Oates' lectures, books, and friendship.

In the dream Pat and I were thrilled, of course, to have Dr. Oates in our home. As he was preparing to leave, I asked him a question: "Wayne, if you could recommend one book to me before you go, what would it be?" In my dream he was holding a little child in his arms (he was very caring and tender toward children as a man, father, and professor). As he approached the door to leave, he said, *Down in the Valley*.

At that point the dream was fading. Just before opening my eyes I wondered, "Who's the author?" That's how the dream ended—with an unanswered question. Then I remembered that I had started recording on paper thoughts about grief after my mini-sabbatical at Duke University Divinity School. The dream inspired me to dust off my notes and to try to finish them under a new title: *Down in the Valley: Our Acquaintance with Grief*.

Through the ages the concept of the valley has been used as a metaphor for both grief and death. This is why Psalm 23 has such a universal appeal. It transcends all belief systems and speaks of an experience all humans encounter: going down into valleys of pain, suffering, grief, and death. During these times the psalmist affirms that certain truths are available. One, the source of our existence is with us in the valleys. Two, the valleys are events within the overall place created by the source of our existence. The place is like a pasture. We are like sheep being led by a shepherd who is with us in and through all of the stages of life (birth, childhood, adolescence, young adulthood, middle age, old age, and death).

Even death is seen as an event in the Good Shepherd's pasture—with an entrance and an exit. All who experience birth will die somewhere in the pasture. Death, however, is not the boundary that ends the pasture. How beautifully this is stated in Psalm 139:7-10:

> Whither shall I go from thy Spirit? Or whither shall I go from thy presence? If I ascend to heaven, thou art there. If I make my bed in Sheol, thou art there! If I take the wings of the morning and dwell in the uttermost part of the sea, even there thy hand shall lead me, and thy right hand shall hold me.

In other words, there is no place in all Creation where we can be that God the Shepherd is not. The universe is his pasture—valleys and all. Then, Jesus domesticates the concept of God: To him, God is not only Shepherd but also Father. As Father, God created humanity in his image (Gen. 1:26). We are therefore more than sheep. We are created as relational beings with a family connection to the Father Creator. Because of the family connection, our identity as humans cannot be solely defined within our humanness. We are created for horizontal relationships—with husbands, wives, brothers, sisters, and other people—and for a custodial relationship to care for all forms of life within a good creation.

But there is a vertical dimension to our identity that touches the identity of who God is. This is true in any parent-child relationship. As our divine parent, God wants to nurture us toward goodness and wholeness. However, the dynamic place where God's identity touches ours requires freedom. Otherwise our identity would be a non-choosing part of God's identity. This would make us echoes of God instead of voices speaking in dialogue and communion. That kind of identity would leave God as a self-contained being turned inward—the very definition of a narcissist. But according to 1 John 4:8, God is love. There was in God, then, a need to create persons who could freely love him back. That is, of course, the risk of parenthood. Children may choose not to love their parents in return.

According to Dr. Pope Duncan, one of my seminary professors and personal friends (now deceased), the history of the world, especially its modern period, is one in which humanity is losing its vertical orientation. Or, as he put it in one of our conversations, "Frank, we are losing our sense of transcendence." And with that loss, we are losing a part of our identity. I contend, therefore, that our world is passing through a valley of collective grief, not because God is dying, but because the world is in a state of mourning from trying to satisfy its vertical selfhood with temporal substitutes. We are in the "far country" as prodigals in denial.

The title I have chosen for this book employs biblical terms to address universal experiences. The term "valley" from Psalm 23 is not the property of a certain religious group; it belongs to humanity and is available to all persons in describing the processes of loss and renewal. The other biblical term in the book's title, "acquainted," also comes from the Old Testament. In Isaiah 53:3 the suffering servant of God is a "man of sorrows, and acquainted with grief." Here, then, is our common ground: our experiences or acquaintance with grief.

The ancient writer shared his losses with his own people, the Jews. Through revealed insight, however, he saw more. He saw common ground where Creator and creation—God and humankind—stand together and process the pain of grief. The central message of the Bible, I believe, is this: "We are not alone in our losses and sorrows." As Isaiah so beautifully says it, "Surely he has born our griefs and carried our sorrows" (53:4a). And again, "Comfort, comfort my people, says your God. Speak tenderly to Jerusalem, and cry to her that her warfare is ended, that her iniquity is pardoned, that she has received from the Lord's hand double for all of her sins" (40:1-2).

It is from this perspective, where God shares with us his own story of grief, that I write. For 52 years as a pastor I have stood with and walked with children, teenagers, and adults through their valleys of sorrow. They have taught me much about grief—theirs and my own. The chapters of this book will reveal some of the lessons and insights I have learned and am still learning. I share them with you in the hope that they will deepen and enrich your relationships as you process your acquaintance with grief in your valley-crossings.

PART ONE
Horizontal Grief

*Even though I walk through the valley of the shadow of death,
I will fear no evil, for thou art with me;
thy rod and staff they comfort me.*
—*Psalm 23:4*

I have chosen to write first about horizontal grief because it is more familiar to us. It involves the losses we experience in our relationships with family members, friends, pets, and valued objects. Other words could be used in describing horizontal grief, such as "finite and temporal."

In other words, as finite beings who live in time between birth and death, we grieve when we lose persons and objects marked by the same limits of time and death. This puts all created beings on the same level—horizontal. Later in this pastoral document we shall deal with another grief zone—vertical, which exists between the Creator and his creation. In it we experience another kind of grief that is both relational and existential. In vertical grief, I will argue that God also grieves but chooses to end his grief differently.

But for now, let's look at horizontal grief as it relates to the stages of life: childhood, adolescence, and adulthood. It may be helpful for you to reflect back on your own childhood and adolescence and remember your particular grief times. What were they? How intense were they? What did you learn about yourself from your losses?

As we mature through the stages of life, our relationship to losses also undergoes a maturing process. In reflecting back on your life, can you affirm your growth in how you process grief? My hope is that as you read about the grief of others cited in this book, you will be inspired to keep growing in your responses to grief. Growth is always possible.

Just as our response to losses is developmental, it also can be a part of our aspirations or longings for the fulfillment of basic human needs. We do grieve as a longing for what is missing and needed in our lives. This is true for all of us, whatever our personal and professional roles may be. I will illustrate this kind of grief with two stories: one about a minister longing for and needing Sabbath rest and the other about a mother who transformed her grief into hope that inspired the creation of a faith community in a new church.

Let's look now at the meaning of horizontal grief.

Grief and Life Stages

We live through developmental stages, from the womb to the tomb, the knowledge upon which we establish and regulate our societal institutions such as our homes, schools, and so on. Our perception of death is also developmental. Erik H. Erikson, in his book, *Insight and Responsibility*, gives an excellent presentation of the developmental nature of the human experiences.

In infancy and early childhood, birth until two years, there is no real concept of death. As a child moves from early childhood into the "playing" stage of age three to four, death is like a place from which someone may return. From this time into school age, children begin to realize that death is real and permanent.

Pat and I remember when our youngest son, Brad, realized when he was about five that death is permanent. We were eating dinner and he began to cry. When I asked him why he was crying, he said, "I don't want to die and you and mom to die." His perception of death was maturing. Our role as his parents was not to stymie that growth, but rather to comfort him by reminding him of our love and faithfulness as we moved together into a good but imperfect future. Brad is now responding to his young son's questions and concerns about death.

During adolescence, death begins to be seen as part of life—albeit a disturbing part. Why, adolescents may ask, would a good God allow people to die? They may get angry when death comes to their families and friends. They may become depressed and blame God, themselves, and others.

As adolescence gives way to young adulthood, death tends to become more distant. Graduations, jobs, careers, weddings, marriage, and new life (offspring) have little place for the grim reaper.

With the onset of middle age, death begins to be experienced in the dynamics of decline. Paul Tournier in his insightful book, *Learning to Grow Old*, states that there are two movements during the human life cycle: the first, from birth to middle age, is on an incline; the second, from middle age to death, is on a decline.[1]

I remember when decline first "hit" my awareness. I looked down at the words of a hymn we were about to sing in a worship service at the First Baptist Church in

Statesboro, Georgia, and the words were blurred. I rubbed my eyes, thinking my vision would clear up. It didn't. At age 43 my journey upward was ending, and my movement downward was beginning.

Both movements, thankfully, occur at a "turtle's pace." And, with sufficient wisdom and maturity, we can start the second movement without, or with a less intense, mid-life crisis. But during our middle years death does begin to appear in the form of decline we experience in our bodies and observe in the growth and decay of mother nature.

In our last stage of life, old age, we face the reality of death. Some people face it with wisdom and integrity. Others tend to face it with varying degrees of disgust and despair. As a pastor, I have ministered to many people as they moved into their valley of the shadow of death. How comforting it is when the normal fear of the process of death and dying is free from the fear of evil by the providential presence of the Good Shepherd.

When my dad, Arles Hawkins, 77, suffering from multiple myeloma, began having double vision in his hospital room, he called a nurse and said, "If I'm dying, I want some of my family with me." The nurse called my sister, Katherine Couick. She and her husband, Bill, were by his side when Dad entered the valley of death. He was not alone. With wisdom, faith, and integrity, Dad embraced in death the same shepherding care that brought him to life through birth.

Through all of the stages of life, from birth to death, from childhood through adulthood, we are sustained by the presence of family and our heavenly Father.

Childhood

Our experiences of grief begin in childhood. It may be the death of a parent, grandparent, or a cherished pet. Children may also feel a deep loss through the divorce of their parents. Consider the following examples of childhood losses.

Losing a family member

In 2016 our youngest son's father-in-law, Tom Reeves, died suddenly from a rupture in his aorta artery. Brad married Tom's step-daughter, Mi Yong Kim, in 2004. Their marriage was blessed with the birth of a boy, Seth, in 2010. Tom, 69, had married Mi Yong's mother, Sung Ji, in South Korea after the death of her first husband in the 1980s. After Tom's tour of duty in the United States Army, he, Sung Ji, and Mi Yong Kim moved to Knoxville, Tennessee. According to Brad, Tom worked in various management positions in retirement, could repair most any kind of machine, and was an excellent cook. In fact, the night before he died, Tom treated Sung Ji, Mi Yong, Brad, and Seth to a delicious dinner prepared on his grill.

Tom's funeral was held at one of Knoxville's funeral homes. Sung Ji's pastor presided over the service and used competently both Korean and English in communicating words of comfort, healing, and hope. A female choral group from the Korean Presbyterian church sang a beautiful hymn. Sung Ji, Mi Yong, Brad, and other immediate family members were seated close to the front where, on an overhead screen, pictures of Tom and family were being presented.

Brad and Mi Yong had asked Pat and me to let Seth sit with us during the service. We were sitting just behind the immediate family (There were several children and family members from Tom's previous marriage in attendance also). Seth, it seemed, was doing well while watching the pictures on the screen.

Because of the sudden and unexpected nature of Tom's death, the first expressions of grief—shock and numbness—were still being mixed with open expressions of emotional pain—the realization that Tom was gone. This was especially true for Sung Ji. She could not hold inside what she felt; she cried a lot.

Seth continued to sit quietly as he saw and heard the images and sounds of grief just ahead of him. At age six he did not understand the full meaning of death. He did know, however, that the people he loved—his grandmother, mother, and dad—were very sad about the absence of his grandfather, and that absence meant he would not be with them anymore. Seth loved his granddad and grieved his loss.

I looked down at Seth and saw tears flowing down his sad face. And in that moment, a moment of providence I would say, Brad and Mi Yong looked back at Seth and motioned for him to come and join them. He did just that with no hesitation. Seth wanted to be in on what his mother, dad, and grandmother were experiencing.

In his young but developing mind, Seth knew he would continue to have the love of his paternal grandparents. He wanted, though, in that moment, to be with the people with whom he had shared his granddad Tom's love on a weekly basis. His acquaintance with grief was fully recognized, and he was in on the immediate family's final "goodbye." That memory of inclusion will stay with Seth and bless him as he matures into adulthood.

As I write about childhood grief, I have three memories of my own sorrow as a child. The first one happened when I was four. My paternal grandfather, Jim Snyder—the only grandparent I had the privilege of knowing—had died. Grandpa Jim had lived with us after Grandmother Mary died on the front porch of our house, holding my brother, Buddy (two years older than I), in her arms. I can still remember my granddad eating at our family table. He made swiping honey on one of Mom's delicious biscuits with a table knife look so yummy. That, with a faded mental picture of the two of us walking in a field near our house, are the only enduring memories I have of being with Grandpa Jim.

I remember being at his graveside service, but I do not remember crying or having feelings of grief. I recall my mother and her family of birth crying and the fact that I was included in that important family event. That memory fits easily into what I keep learning about relationships and their centrality in what is truly valuable.

My second memory of childhood grief relates to a loss when I was 12. My oldest brother, Virgil, and his wife, Ruby, were expecting a baby. Virgil was one of the fortunate ones who had survived the horrors of the Second World War. He had served as a tracer gunner on the *USS Bunker Hill*, a medium-sized aircraft carrier, in the war against Japan. He and Ruby were doing what a multitude of post-war couples were doing: catching up on love-making (many of whom had parenthood in mind).

I remember so well the evening little Arnold was born. Virgil took Ruby to the York County Hospital around 4 p.m. I was planning to attend a softball game at 7 o'clock. About 6:30 the exciting news came: it's a boy! We were filled with joy. Little Arnold was the first grandchild to bless the Hawkins family. And, I, at 12, had the distinct honor of becoming an uncle. I went to the game and shared the Hawkins' joy with my friends and received with pride their congratulations—"Hello, Uncle Frank!"

After the game I ran home to get the latest word about little Arnold, Virgil, and Ruby. When I entered the sitting room I knew something was wrong. Mom, Dad, Kat (my older sister), and Buddy were not celebrating. Mom and Kat were crying. Dad and Buddy had sadness written on their faces. I asked, "What's wrong?" Dad answered, "Frank, little Arnold didn't make it. There were complications, and he died at birth."

I was shocked. I had never felt such joy and grief in such a short span of time. I was an uncle, and then I wasn't. Virgil and Ruby were parents, and then they were childless. I wanted to be alone. Men in our family didn't cry together, so I ran to the back bedroom and cried like a baby. I was still a child, but I felt profound grief.

After that experience I could never believe that children are better off being protected or shielded from grief. They do grieve and are capable of growing through owning their sorrow and being included in the family response to losses. There may be, however, some health and family dynamics that may necessitate some degree of shielding. These, I believe, are rare. My being involved in our family grief made my joy even greater when, 18 months later, Ruby gave birth to a healthy boy. Often, joy does follow grief and may be deepened and enriched when they are experienced as partners in the unfolding of our imperfect, finite lives.

My acquaintance with grief, however, started in early childhood as I related to and was impacted by the sorrows of my mother and father. Mom, the baby in her family of seven children, still grieved over the death of her mother who died several years before my birth. Mom and her three sisters and three brothers adored their mother. My sister, two brothers, and I experienced our mother's grief in her emotional battles to become a mature person without her mother's strength and counsel. At times our relationship with Mom was joyful; she knew how to be playful and spontaneous. We saw that side of her quite often at the family table where she served delicious meals.

For example, one Saturday evening when I was about six, mom served us some of her piping hot oyster stew. Suddenly it happened: she opened a box of saltine crackers that had been in the pantry for days, and out jumped a little mouse! From the box to mom's individual bowl (already filled with scalding hot stew), the mouse splashed to a sudden death. And just as suddenly, Mom fell to the floor. After we gave the mouse a quick burial via the back door, and retrieved Mom from her fall, we had a beautiful time of fellowship and laughter.

That event is permanently lodged in our family's memory place. Along with the spontaneity and humor, I was also impacted by mom's unresolved grief, complicated by the onset of menopause, that I felt but did not understand as a child.

My dad's grief was more complex. When I moved into my mid-teens, I began to experience a grief that was difficult to explain. I felt lonely. I had a good family and lots of friends, and yet, something was missing. My feelings of relational distance were especially acute between Dad and me. He was one of the best men I have ever known. But I did not feel close to him. All through childhood that was my experience of our relationship: distance.

My relationship with Mom was different. She was talkative, at times too much so. And yet, all four of us children could dialogue with her—arguing, discussing, and joking. I often said that Mom never had a thought she didn't share! With Dad, it was a matter of listening but not much dialogue. We respected him as a good, honest, and decent man. Emotionally, however, I did not feel masculine warmth in our relationship.

In my late teens and through my college years I felt resentment toward Dad. People in our community would say, "Frank, you are like your dad; you even look like him." On the inside I rejected those comparisons. I did not want to be like him; and yet, I loved and respected my dad and was like him. I internalized those feelings and shared them with no one. At times I wanted to shout at Dad and say something like, "Dad, let's have a good conversation and disagree and talk back and forth and, then, laugh about it." We didn't have that kind of relationship, and I knew it.

At age 16, of course, I was not able to understand the interpersonal dynamics that existed between Dad and me. I was too focused on my own pain to understand his. Later I came to see life, my dad, and myself differently. I began to see our relationship as a part of our family system and stream. He was born west of Asheville, North Carolina, in 1900. His mother died shortly after his birth. His father and only sibling, a brother, died when he was in middle childhood. My dad was acquainted with much grief as a child. Grandparents, aunts, and uncles reared him and gave him a stable and caring home. Dad carried his grief, however, throughout his entire life.

In my 30s I was able to forgive him for what he was unable to give to me. He really did not need my forgiveness. He had been to Mom and his children a very responsible husband and father. He gave to us the very best of what he had received. Along with that best, however, we received his unresolved grief over losing his nuclear family in early and middle childhood. And we discovered that Judith Viorst is right when in her book, *Necessary Losses*, she says something like this: Sometimes the losses of early childhood may continue to dwell within us all of our lives.[2]

I was impacted by Dad's early childhood losses and internalized them as the way fathers and sons are supposed to relate. But something in me just didn't feel right. Then I came to realize I was experiencing (without knowing it) some of Dad's early childhood feelings of distance and detachment from his mother and family still alive in him and in our father-son relationship. This also complicated my relationship with the fatherhood of God.

I had been taught by my church and family that God was our heavenly Father. My experience of fatherhood had been one of dependability and distance. I had been baptized when I was 10 years old. Six years later, though, I was experiencing both of my fathers as being distant. I grieved over both relationships.

One evening in the spring of that year I was home alone. The aloneness I felt, though, was on the inside. I felt distant from God. At times in the past I had felt closer, but that had faded. Then I did something I had not done in years. I knelt by the sofa and prayed, "God, I'm not getting up from here until I get through to you." I had never spoken to God that way. What kind of response would I get? Silence? Anger? Rebuke?

The response blew me away with a sense of joy! No voices. No rushing wind. There was a quiet, ineffable sense of peace. It was like an emotional and spiritual dam bursting, with cleansing and healing waters rushing in to fill the vacuum I felt on the inside. To me, I had challenged God to be intimate and he responded (non-verbally) "What took you so long?"

That night I was blessed to some degree like Jacob, who at the ford of the Jabbok challenged God to bless him (see Gen. 32:24-32). I have learned, however, that "breakthroughs" are never "arrival stations" to any form of perfection. My acquaintance with my parents' grief would continue to live in me. The blessing I received that night in 1952 set me free to accept not only their grief in me but also their joy—my mother's spontaneity and my dad's solitude.

Two gifts, though created from our imperfect family history, are, I believe, the reliable stuff out of which authentic ministry may come. Someone has said that we need to accept our past as non-negotiable. When we do, the treasure of our past, though imperfect, can be set free to bless our present and future lives. Not accepting our past may cause us to make of it a valley of unresolved grief and a place where we miss the joy of a better future.

Dealing with divorce

Betty Jordan left a message with my secretary for me to call her. She had gone through a painful divorce from her husband the previous year and had custody of their two children, Bob, 11, and Jenny, 8. When I called Betty I could hear the pain in her voice as she said, "Pastor, Bob and Jenny are becoming unmanageable. I can't cope with being a mother and father. Could you please see me?"

We set up a time for her to come to my study at the church. Betty was still in her valley of grief. She was hurting and angry with Robert, who after 22 years walked away from their marriage. She shared with me her frustrations about working at her job eight hours a day and then having to be both parents to Bob and Jenny. Following is the conversation I had with Betty:

Betty: At times I feel like walking away from Bob and Jenny, too.
Pastor: What keeps you from doing that, Betty?
Betty: If I didn't love them so much, maybe I could (begins to cry).
Pastor: Betty, I've never known the kind of hurt you feel. I've had my own hurts, and I want to stand with you in yours.
Betty: Thank you (looking up with Kleenex in hand).
Pastor: Let me see if I heard you correctly. Did you say Robert walked away from Bob and Jenny?
Betty: Well, he's not around much (her neck becomes red).
Pastor: Does he offer to be with Bob and Jenny?

Betty: Oh yes, but I don't think that is good for them. If we're not going to be a family, we need to get on with our lives.
Pastor: Betty, do you still love Robert?
Betty: (She begins to sob. She cries for several minutes). I'm sorry. I do still love him and, yet, I know it's over. (pause) What can I do?
Pastor: Betty, you are being a very responsible mother to your children in spite of the fact that you are still grieving a loss you did not want. My hunch is that Bob and Jenny miss their dad also and need to spend more time with him. What ever the future brings to you and Robert, Bob and Jenny need and want both of you and your love. And you, too, need that kind of support.
Betty: It will be awkward and difficult, but I'm willing to try. (pause) Pastor, Bob and Jenny need to talk to someone. They do have feelings of hurt, and I don't know how to handle it. Would you spend some time with them?
Pastor: I'll be glad to see them. Why don't you talk to them and see if they are ready to talk with me?
Betty: Thanks, I will.

The following Wednesday after the evening prayer service I met with Jenny and Bob in my study. They agreed to come but seemed reluctant. As we talked, I remembered some of my own hurts when I was their age—the relationship pain I experienced with my father and the grief of being separated from Virgil, my brother, during the Second World War. My hurts were different, but I could understand Bob and Jenny's pain. They were quiet and seemed nervous as they entered my study.

Pastor: Hello, Jenny and Bob. How are things going for you?
Jenny: OK, I guess. Bob and I just can't seem to get along together.
Bob: Jenny, why do you have to talk about that? You always talk too much.
Jenny: Well, it's true (Bob turns away from Jenny).
Pastor: Is this the way things go for you around the house?
Jenny: Most of the time, Bob thinks he has to be the boss now that Daddy's gone (Bob doesn't respond).
Pastor: How do you feel about your daddy being gone? (Bob turns to my bookshelf and reaches for a book.). You miss your dad, don't you? (Bob nods up and down as tears flow down his cheeks. Jenny looks at Bob and cries also. I listened). When I was your age I had some hurts in my family; I cried, too. You have a right to your tears, both of you, and so does your mother. She has been hurt deeply and has been trying to do a lot for both of you. I believe she is beginning to accept the fact that you need her and your dad. It won't be easy; it will take all of you helping each other. How do you feel about that?
Bob: I'll do my part (smiling for the first time).
Jenny: Me, too!
Pastor: Thanks for coming, Jenny and Bob. I think your mother will be ready to talk with you and your dad about a definite schedule of visits with him.

I met with Betty, Bob, and Jenny for subsequent visits over the next several years. I watched them come out of their valley of grief and trust people, life, and God more fully. Although Robert and Betty were not reconciled, they established a plan of mutual parental care and leadership for their children. Bob and Jenny grew into their teens having both parents present in their lives. The eternal Shepherd had been with them in their valley—crossing, in spirit, and through their church's care.

Children do grieve and need to have their grief recognized and accepted by the adults to whom they look for guidance and care, as evidenced in this concluding illustration:

A graduate of Southern Seminary and his son, three, and daughter, five, were on a plane returning from the funeral of his wife and his children's mother. The family sat in silence for a while. Then, realizing he had been more focused on his own grief than his children's, John said, "Sue and Bob, I know how much you loved your mother. And, I want you to know it was nothing you did that caused her to die."

After a brief silence Sue looked up at John and asked, "Daddy, do you know how to cook?" John had recognized his children's grief and any feelings of guilt they may have had about her death. He was saying to his children, "We're in this valley together, and life will go on. I can't take your mother's place, but I can cook and we'll come out of our valley together."

Children need and deserve to hear messages of reassurance when they grieve.

Teen Years

Teenagers may appear to be too busy with growing up to have time for losses. Then it happens: the death of a role model or the slow demise of a friend whose burden they help to carry. Let's explore some examples of teenage grief.

Losing a role model

I entered Rock Hill High School in 1949. During those days the school was famous in South Carolina for producing state championship football teams. Under the leadership of Coach Walter Jenkins, assisted by Coach Gene Avery and Coach Mack McCall, that had occurred twice—in 1946 and 1947. In 1949 the Bearcats were expected, once again, to be one of the top teams in the Palmetto State. One of the main reasons for that expectation was a running back named Hal Saverance.

Hal was not only a powerful running back, but also a role model for those of us who were freshmen and sophomores. Besides that, he was a good-looking guy. Hal, after his senior year, entered the University of South Carolina on a football scholarship. In 1952 he made a trip back to Rock Hill, planning to take his girlfriend, Ann Polk, a student at Rock Hill High, to the junior-senior prom.

Before the prom Hal and a friend, Sonny Davis, decided to go fishing below the dam that crossed the Catawba River. I don't remember the details about what happened, but I do remember the shock and grief that gripped the entire student body, faculty, and town when we heard that Hal had drowned in the swift-flowing water below the dam.

I did not attend Hal's funeral service held at the First Presbyterian Church, but one of my good friends, John Jackson, did attend. In fact, he was part of a quartet who sang a special arrangement of "Sunset and Evening Star" from Tennyson's poem "Crossing the Bar." The church, I heard, was filled with Hal's family and Rock Hill High School faculty members and students.

To this day a memory lingers with me: the uncanny, collective silence in the halls of our school that seemed to say "We shouldn't be here in this valley of grief. We should be at the football field, watching Hal score touchdowns, or, in the decorated gym watching Hal dance with Ann at the junior-senior prom." But there we were, facing the reality of death, and a whisper of our own mortality, and the realization that death can happen anytime—from infancy to ripe old age. And, yes, death can invade and interrupt high school dreams and plans.

Can there be a value, then, in such untimely and unwelcomed grief? Could it be this: To not clutch life possessively, but, to receive it as a gift every day with the open hands of gratitude, knowing that without the mysterious and wondrous gift of God's grace, we would not be here at all?

Sharing the burden

Susan Jones was a vivacious 18-year-old teenager. She lived with her family in a modest five-room house in Louisville, Kentucky's eastside. She had one sister, Joan, age 15. Their parents were "home bodies" but made sure their girls were included in church activities. One day Susan went to see her medical doctor, complaining about abdominal pain. After a series of tests she was diagnosed with pancreatic cancer. Susan and her family had a valley to cross. They scheduled treatments and Susan responded to them well, but her condition gradually deteriorated, resulting in increasing pain.

My role as their pastor was to walk with them through their valley and to call forth people resources to share their journey with them. This is one of the blessings of belonging to a community of faith: we are not alone when crises come. Susan and her family were not alone. We were with them as burden-sharers.

A part of our being with them took the form of listening to their pain without passing judgment or trying to analyze it. At times the family members sounded like Job: They cried out to God, "Why Susan and why now? She's only 18." We had no answers. We just kept going and listening.

Some of our men gave help. Some of our women took food. Some of our teenagers visited and were there when the valley became darker and more fearsome. At times we heard Jesus' cry from the cross "My God, My God, why have you forsaken me?" (Matt. 27:46). We had no answers. We just kept caring for and walking with the Jones family in their valley.

I'll never forget visiting Susan in the hospital as she neared the end of her life. Her pain medicine was suppressing her suffering, and there was a hint of her vivacious self in her pale face. Several of her teenage friends were there. I stayed for a while, had prayer, and was ready to leave them to their peer conversation. Susan gave me a gift in that moment, though, that I will always cherish. She said, "Dr. Hawkins, don't go. We are going to have a party, and you are invited." Susan loved Tootsie Rolls. She had sent several of her friends to purchase some for a party. I stayed and we ate Tootsie Rolls and managed to laugh together with Susan.

Susan and her friends had invited me to be with them at a tender moment in their lives. It happened because our church had been family to the Jones in a time of crisis. Susan died that evening. Over the next several days we gathered with her family to remember and celebrate her life. Grieving people can celebrate in the midst of their tears when they are sustained by the presence of the eternal Shepherd. The "Thou art with us" would call both Susan and us from the valley to restored living. He would walk with her through the valley of death and with us through the valley of grief.

The Apostle Paul becomes our counselor during our experiences of grief, saying "But we would not have you ignorant, brethren, concerning those who are asleep, that you may not grieve as others do who have no hope" (1 Thess. 4:13). On one hand, he gives us permission to grieve. Failure to grieve in the face of loss would be unnatural. On the other hand, he gives us permission to celebrate with hope—even with Tootsie Rolls, I believe.

Adulthood

As we move into our adult years, our grief experiences may become more numerous—the deaths of spouses, aging parents, grandparents, and close friends and the loss of health and jobs. At times these losses may produce unresolved grief complicated by depression and anger. Some people may experience unresolved grief as a longing for a place.

Dealing with unresolved grief

In each of the five churches I served I knew families who had difficulty with unresolved grief. Some, I believe, became trapped by denial of past hurts and may have refocused their anger toward others—what someone has called "delivering the mail to the wrong address." Often ministers, lay people, and family members become targets where unresolved grief is inappropriately discharged. I remember such a case in one of my pastorates.

When I became pastor of the church I was told, "Watch out for Mrs. Jones: she'll give you plenty of trouble." Quite frankly, I had no desire to engage her in conversational combat. One day, however, it happened. Our church secretary buzzed me on the intercom and said, "Mrs. Jones is here to see you." A feeling of dread possessed me as I responded, "Send her in."

When Mrs. Jones entered my office, she didn't sit down. Her attack began from a standing position. "How could you let the voting go the way it did in our last business meeting?" She was referring to a certain decision made by the church. Her vote on the issue had been cast with a small minority. It was obvious that she was not happy about the decision made by the majority.

I weighed her words, "How could *you* let the voting go the way it did?" She had placed me in a defensive position, and, of course, I wanted to defend myself. The church had voted freely without pressure from anyone. I had not let anything happen; the church had let it happen. I felt anger churning in my stomach and wanted to stand up and attack her just as loudly as she had attacked me. If I had done that, however, my loudness and hers would have been an exercise in mutual rejection. That would have been a lose-lose conclusion.

As I sat looking up at Mrs. Jones, I made a decision to be her pastor—not her target—so I asked, "Virginia, is something bothering you that I can help you with?"

The fact that I didn't attack her back seemed to surprise her. She sat down and began to cry and share with me about the death of her husband three years earlier. She said, "Pastor, I've been so lonely since Jim died; life is just not the same when you live in a house by yourself."

In that moment I saw a hurting lady who apparently had lived with unresolved anger in her family. I had heard her cry and was able to give her comfort instead of ongoing rejection. She and I became good friends. I'm not sure her grief was over, but at least her pattern of attack had been temporarily broken, which was a sign of what could be.

Hope for Mrs. Jones and for all of us who live in families comes, in great measure, from coming to terms with our own family histories, with all of their pluses and minuses, and with all of their losses and gains. Healthy families are not free from losses but are courageous enough to live with and through their losses. They are not willing to make their collective past a dwelling place, but rather, a launching place toward a future of growth and mutuality.

Coming to terms with our family losses requires a resolute patience, staying focused on the hurt, and firmly believing that healing is possible. Some family members may seek to bypass the pain of family losses and thus settle for lives of nagging, chronic, unresolved grief. Others tend to face the pain of the losses and emerge healthier, happier, and more mature.

Longing for a place

John appeared at our home about 2 p.m. one afternoon. He had an unusual request: "Pastor Frank, will you help me to get to the United States?" John and I had one thing in common: both of us had come to Brazil from other countries. My family and I had arrived in Brazil in 1966 as missionaries. John had come to Brazil in 1949 from Hungary. He had been exiled from his country by the Communist regime.

I listened intently as he shared his story. He had been a governmental official in Hungary. When the Communists came to power in his country, he lost his job and had to flee from his hometown. His family was imprisoned and never heard from again. Along with many others, John left his country in order to remain alive. Later he made his way to Brazil and had lived there for about 17 years. Being in his late 70s, John's longings to have contact with home had intensified. The only member of his family alive, to his knowledge, was a nephew who had emigrated to the United States. That nephew represented to John a family, a home, and a place.

I tried to help John, but after talking with persons at the U.S. embassy in Sao Paulo, I realized that John's chances of going to the United States were almost nil. He would have to have a solid promise of a job in the States before he could receive the necessary documents, so I wrote to several friends in the United States about job possibilities for John. Their companies, however, did not need the liability of a man in the evening years of his human potential. John remained in Brazil, and I'm sure enjoyed a degree of happiness, for I found him to be a relational person. But his memories of significant persons and places, which are a part of the process of growing up and older, brought him pain. He was homesick for the places he remembered.

We identify with John, because a part of being human is seeking places in life. Paul Tournier in his book, *A Place for You*, speaks of this quest. According to Dr. Tournier, a Swiss doctor and devoted Christian, to be human is to seek places to be. What is this seeking process all about? It has to do with happiness, rest, creativity, fulfillment, acceptance, and appreciation. These human longings and others are attached to geographical, vocational, and relational places in our lives.[3]

Geographical places shape our lives more than we may realize. This truth became quite real to me in the fall of 1977. Pat and I had gone to Atlanta for a convention. In the midst of joyful fellowship a message of grief came to us. My father had died about seven o'clock that morning. He had been ill with cancer for several years. We had gone through periods of anticipatory grief during the months of his decline. The actual death had finally come. After calling our children in Statesboro and arranging for them to travel with my in-laws, Pat and I left Atlanta, bound for Rock Hill, South Carolina, the place of our births.

Grief does a large portion of its healing work in the dimension of memory. We found that to be true as we traveled along Interstate 85. Around noon we passed through Greenville. Our grief and memory identified with that place. Both Pat and I had attended college there. She had gone to North Greenville Junior College. I had attended Furman University.

In my grief I remembered my father's many sacrifices that had made possible my college education. Without his parental care, plus that of my mother, Greenville may have been just another piece of geography through which we passed thoughtlessly. But as we journeyed through that Piedmont city under a bright November sun, it was with a sense of familiarity. Suddenly, we felt at home. The very geography, bound up in our common memories, reached out to comfort our wounded spirits.

From Greenville to Rock Hill we passed by more sights that gave us a sense of being in place. Oak trees growing tall like quiet sentinels, straw fields rimmed by honeysuckle thickets, red clay banks causing the landscape to blush with intermittent surprise—these geographical traits and others became nature's hand of comfort reaching out to touch us. We were not strangers in a distant place. The geography that had been our birth and growth places became our minister as we made our way toward family and friends.

I can understand why the Jews from generation to generation have looked toward Jerusalem in times of tears, terror, and celebration. It has been and remains their geographical place. They are no different from us. Deep within us there is a need for a place, a place to be and with which we can identify human emotions. Surely God has put that longing in us.

The longing, however, is not just geographical in nature. It is also vocational. We need a place to be, vocationally. People speak of this need in various ways. At times someone will say, "I'm looking for my place in life." Or, someone may ask the question, "Where is my niche in life?" In this manner we speak of our place, our place of being at home vocationally. There is nothing, I'm convinced, that can make a person happier than to have the feeling, "I've found my place in life."

A significant vocational place seeks to fulfill at least two human needs. First, there is the economic need. Our world functions according to economic principles and standards. There is nothing wrong with an appropriate concern for economic advancement and justice in seeking one's vocational place.

Second, there is the need to fulfill our creative gifts. Here we must listen to the spirit within, the creative spirit. If the spirit of an artist, poet, singer, prophet, doctor, lawyer, or other professional lives within, we should release it through adequate preparation and dedication.

Children and young people should realize that arriving at their vocational place is both gift and achievement. The gift emerges from the form of raw materials and resources. The achievement comes from long hours of careful and dedicated preparation in which the raw materials become refined and ready for service. There are persons who never arrive at their vocational place because they see that place only as gift and not as a process of developmental growth.

So it is with us. Our human spirits brood over our inner space and see there the struggle between creation and chaos, form and formlessness. Vocational courage calls us to see the pattern of creativity within and to bring it forth as an act of vocational achievement. When such courage is rooted in self-giving love, our vocational place becomes a joyful place to be. It is joyful because, being created in God's image, we have a need to give that which is received, valued, appreciated, and shared by other persons. It is in such giving that we discover the meaning of fulfilled personhood.

I return now to my Hungarian friend John. He missed his geographical and vocational places, to be sure. The main place for which he felt homesick, however, was his relational place. This is why, I'm sure, he wanted to see his nephew—his only living relative. This does not mean that John had not established other significant friendships. He had. In old age, however, one returns to that relational place called family. John was doing a natural thing.

Again, we identify with John. We have a place in the lives of people. That place ultimately gives meaning to both geography and vocation. If our relational place is creative and fulfilling, it can transform our physical surroundings and our vocational commitments and cause them to be happy places. Our relational place is ever with us; it is the ability to relate to other persons with accepting and creative interpersonal love.

We begin choosing our relational places during the teenage years. During those growth years we do much choosing. This is the meaning of peer groups, having sweethearts, going steady, transacting the engagement, and, finally, getting married. These are choices through which we establish the relational places that are populated with chosen persons. Or, if we opt for singleness, then our relational places are filled with persons from the perspective of singlehood. In finding our relational places, we know that deep within we are following the pattern of God's own personhood. God, too, chooses persons to fill his marvelous creation.

The greatest truth, therefore, about our longing for a place is this: our most significant place is a person. The Bible puts it in beautiful relational terms. "Lord: thou hast been our dwelling place in all generations" (Ps. 90:1). This means that when we know the meaning of self-giving love, we are dwelling in an everlasting place that is a person. For, "God is love, and he who abides in love abides in God, and God abides in him" (1 John 4:16). To dwell in love that knows how to give as blessing is to dwell in God.

My friend John did not return to his relational place symbolized by his nephew. He had access, though, to a person in whom he could abide in a foreign land. He knew the Lord, who is our everlasting place.

Notes

[1] Paul Tournier, *Learning to Grow Old* (New York: Harper and Row, 1972), 9.
[2] Judith Viorst, *Necessary Losses* (New York: Ballantine Books, 1986), 283.
[3] Paul Tournier, *A Place for You* (New York: Harper and Row, 1968), 9-24.

Grieving for Sabbath Rest

The church was shocked by Dr. Smith's resignation. He stood and read it to the congregation during the Sunday morning worship service. It would take effect immediately. "What went wrong?" everyone asked. He seemed to have it all. He was young, only 45, and at the peak of what appeared to be an outstanding career. His messages were well prepared and dynamically delivered. His wife and two children were well integrated into the life of the community and the church. He was a good listener and counseled many of the church's members, especially young couples and their children. The weddings and funerals he conducted were very relational, and he had been elected to a key responsibility in one of his denomination's most important agencies. He seemed to handle all of these opportunities with grace and ease.

What appeared to be true, however, was not. On a Friday evening Dr. Smith met with the church's key leaders and shared his inner pain:

> I haven't slept well for more than a year now. I have to drag myself from one duty to another. I have stopped being creative and feel like I just react to the next unexpected thing that comes along. My fatigue doesn't show: I've learned to hide it in the pulpit and in public. In those areas people expect me to smile and be positive. At home, however, Jane and the children see the real me. They know how burned out and weary I am, and they know who gets my leftover energies: they do. I can't continue like this. Therefore, I will resign this Sunday, effective immediately. I'm not sure what my next step will be.

This kind of professional breakdown is very common in modern society. It is present in all professions, but especially in those that deal with caring for people. An overload of stress is often the culprit behind such crises. Those of us who have been in Dr. Smith's shoes will agree that stress is a factor in professional burnout. I believe, though, that there is a more basic factor we may be missing.

Sam Keen in his book, *Inward Bound*, deals with this factor in an insightful manner. He states that prior to the Industrial Revolution, people lived with the rhythm of the seasons. The decline of fall and winter were seen as stages in the ebb and flow of life—all life, including people. With the coming of the machine, however, the rhythm of human life changed. The machine doesn't operate according to seasons. For the sake of productivity, its cycle admits only spring and summer. Keen contends that modern man has adapted to the rhythm of the machine and has internalized it as his own. I call this adaptation "worshipping the god of two seasons." This kind of idolatry cannot bypass decline; instead, it produces premature decline, or burnout.[1]

And yet, we try to hide decline and cover it up. Dr. Smith did. Multitudes of us attempt to dismiss it as we see its first signs in early middle age. We begin to need glasses, have less stamina, cannot retain factual data as easily as we did earlier, and do not have the sexual potency we once had. Our tendency is to hide these signs of decline or to even deny their existence.

Churches can worship this false god of two seasons also. Baptist churches are especially given to the avoidance of fall and winter in their cycles of institutional life. Productivity becomes the goal of the machine-like churches, believing they should stay in a perpetual state of revival (spring) and productivity (summer). Decline is seen as evil. Ministers are expected to lead the churches in a dynamic cycle of never-ending activities and programs that demonstrates the power of God is in the churches. When decline comes—and it will—laity place guilt and blame on the clergy, and vice versa. Forced terminations and premature resignations often occur so the churches can cease declining and experience a new spiritual springtime.

Fortunately for Dr. Smith, he confessed that he was in a period of decline. The church responded with compassion to his self-disclosure. When he shared his resignation, one of the respected elders of the church stood and said, "I move that we give Dr. Smith a sabbatical—whatever time he needs to rest and get his batteries recharged. I further move that we include in our church budget funds to cover periodic sabbaticals for our pastor and our other ministers so this kind of crisis might be prevented in the future." The motion received unanimous approval. Dr. Smith was heard in his confession of professional despair, and given a season for rest and replenishment.

I can only wish that this might become the case for numerous ministers and other professionals who grieve in private before a god of two seasons. I do not know how other professionals respond to unrealistic expectations. I do know, however, how ministers tend to respond: They live with varying degrees of chronic depression, experience health breakdowns, lose their jobs because of pain-relieving sexual adventures, leave the ministry over role-expectation conflicts, move to other churches to obtain an institutional honeymoon that will fade all too quickly under the crushing load of a two-season philosophy of church growth, or just hunker down and endure the boredom.

My hope is that more churches will begin to practice preventive medicine for their ministers by providing them planned replenishment seasons. It should not take a crisis for churches to practice what the Bible teaches us about our humanity. When God finished Creation, he instituted the Sabbath and two seasons, fall and winter, in recognition of Creation's need to be restored.

All aspects of Creation need these down times so that the exhaustible forces within can be restored in authentic renewal. If fall and winter are bypassed, spring and summer will lose their potency. Not only is this vital for ministers; it is essential for the well-being of churches and other institutions. Instead of anxiously trying to stay in a perpetual season of revival and productivity, churches could be blessed by having sabbaticals from revivals and large-scale activities or programs.

The god of two seasons would have us believe that unless we are in productive revival, we are dead as persons, churches, and institutions. This deception has gotten us out of rhythm. The truth is this: Unless we accept decline and dormancy, fall and winter, as part of our rhythm, we will become like dead people in the midst of machine-like revivals and activities. The prophet Isaiah saw it this way:

> Have you not known? Have you not heard? The Lord is the everlasting God, the Creator of the ends of the earth. He does not faint or grow weary. His understanding is unsearchable. He gives power to the faint, and to him who has no might He increases strength. Even youths shall faint and be weary, and young men shall fall exhausted; but they who wait for the Lord shall renew their strength, they shall mount up with wings like eagles. They shall run and not be weary, they shall walk and not faint. (Isa. 40-28-31)

The Creator does not faint or grow weary. All of us—including ministers, church members, and secular institutions—do. This is not a sin; neither is it a weakness. In accepting our weariness and decline as natural, and in waiting on the Eternal One in our Sabbath times, our strength is renewed for soaring, running, and walking.

Note

[1] Sam Keen, *Inward Bound* (New York: Bantam Books, 1992), 16-35.

The Power of Hope

People respond to their grief differently. Some choose to dream dreams as a way to transform losses into blessings. Others find a way to trust in spite of painful suffering and losses. Some find comfort in God's sustaining grace that gives hope to emerge from their particular valleys of sorrow.

Dreams Emerging From Loss

Malinda Minervo Black was born west of Asheville, North Carolina, on August 10, 1852, the daughter of Alfred and Polly Martin Black. When "Lindy" was seven years old, her father was killed by a falling tree while cutting flax on their farm in the Alexander community. Her mother died when she was 11. Two of her father's brothers came from Ellijay, Georgia, and took Lindy to live with their families. The long difficult trip on horseback occurred during the winter months. When they reached Ellijay, Lindy's feet had been so traumatized by the cold weather that she was unable to walk for weeks.

But with the passing of time, the little mountain girl recovered and began attending school. One of her classmates was a girl from a well-to-do family. She befriended Lindy and shared with her wheat biscuits at lunchtime. That was quite a treat during the tragic days of the Civil War when food was often scarce and fighting was nearby. Lindy and her classmates heard the cannons roar during the battle of Atlanta.

Later, Lindy's friend invited her to a revival at the Methodist church where she and her family attended. On the last night of the revival meeting, her friend made a profession of faith in Jesus Christ. In that same evening Lindy made a decision to accept Christ and experience Christian baptism. Sharing friendship and bread with an orphan led to Lindy's embracing Christianity and a life filled with self-giving service. Children can encourage and bless.

When Lindy was 17 she returned to the Alexander community in North Carolina to live with relatives. There she met John Sluder, whom she married and with whom she had 16 children. When Lindy was 33 she began to have dreams of a church that would serve God and the people in their small community. One night she had a vision in which she saw a church on the hill behind their house. The dream was very vivid, with scenes of worship, baptisms, weddings, and a cemetery. The vision so excited Lindy that she awakened John and shared it with him.

"John, will you give me that piece of land to start a church?" she asked. John agreed and promised four acres for her holy project. When Lindy shared her vision with the people of the community, some laughed, a few believed, but most thought building a church on the hillside impossible. She quietly went about her life, nurturing the vision.

Grief, with which Lindy had been intimately acquainted since childhood, would once again be a challenging force in her life. Her baby, Arrie Elizabeth, died. She, John, and their family entered a time of mourning. "Where are we going to bury her?" John asked Lindy. With a heavy heart but resolute spirit, Lindy replied: "Why, on the hill, where the church cemetery will be." The community gathered with Lindy and John on the hill. There, amid silent, watching mountains, they lowered Arrie's body into the first grave of the church's cemetery.

Then, entering Lindy's dream, they began to hew logs, and donate time and timber to build a church house. From that visionary and courageous beginning, Mountain View Baptist Church has served its community for more than 100 years. On the hill people have come to worship, baptize believers, celebrate weddings, and bury their dead.

Lindy Sluder continued to participate in the church's activities until she died in November 1938. When she became ill and could not sit on the hard pews, she asked, "Do you think they'd think hard of me if I took my rocking chair to church so I can sit near the choir and hear the music?" No one minded in the least. For two years Lindy sat at the front and listened to the music and sermons. When she knew she could no longer sit in her chair, Lindy asked that it be left in the church for any old or sick person who might need it.

The chair is still there. It is a reminder of how dreams and hope can emerge from loss and grief. Lindy was my dad's grandmother. I did not have the opportunity to know my great-grandmother Lindy. Yet, I feel blessed by being downstream as a member of her family. She took what she could not prevent—being an orphan—and transformed her grief into a life where vision became her vocation. Perhaps my dad learned from her mentoring influence how to cope with his grief. He, too, became an orphan as a child.

I can still imagine him as a child, playing along the mountain stream that flowed by his grandmother's house. One day he tried to jump across that creek, but didn't make it. That evening he placed his wet brogans on the hearth by the fire. The next morning instead of being dry, they were burned beyond use. Back then, children received one pair of shoes a year. My dad went barefooted that year well into the frost zone of autumn.

Before he was re-shoed with the rest of his siblings, he had to do his job of rounding up the cows for feeding and milking. One of his aunts said that little Arles would run out to the pasture where the cows were reclining and kick one up and stand on the warm, vacated ground. That image of my dad will always be a treasured memory. He was acquainted with much grief, as was his grandmother, Lindy. However, they did not give up hope. They learned how to find the warmth they needed. So must we.

Trust Emerging from Suffering

The book of Job has the reputation of being one of the oldest books of the Bible. The author tells a story about a man and his wife who face mysterious and massive suffering. The storyteller makes sure his readers understand that Job is an upright, God-fearing, blameless man—one of the greatest people of his day. He also has an abundance of sheep, camels, oxen, she-asses, and servants. This rich man is so good that after the parties of his children (seven sons and three daughters), he makes burnt offerings and sends up prayers in case they might have sinned against God.

After that quick summary about the main character's virtues and greatness, the author leaves Job and transports his audience to God's presence where God's sons are being presented, and Satan comes among them. (Back then, Satan was adversarial but acted only as God gave him permission.) God asks Satan a question about his travels. "Where have you been?" He answers, "To and fro on the earth."

God praises Job's virtues and asks Satan if he has observed Job and seen what an upright man he is. Satan argues that Job is good only because God has placed a hedge of protection around him, his family, and his possessions. Remove the hedge and see what Job does: He'll curse you and reveal his true nature. God enters an agreement with Satan to test the authenticity of Job's goodness. It sounds like a wager: God betting on the reliability of Job's goodness and Satan betting that Job's goodness will flunk the test of suffering and loss.

Then, quickly the author brings his audience back from God's presence where he has authorized Satan to test Job's goodness. The scene is once again on earth where Job lives. He is unaware of what is about to "hit" him. And, more importantly, he is unaware of what has happened at God's throne between God and Satan. What if someone had said something like this to him?

"Job, God and Satan got together and made an agreement to test the depth of your goodness. God believes you will remain true and good in the face of suffering and grief. Satan thinks your goodness is a fake that will vanish when suffering and loss come your way." (Job, I'm sure, would have appreciated the foreknowledge.)

Like Job, we face suffering—often without warning, out of the blue . . .

- the sudden death of a spouse
- the first pain of terminal cancer that has been eating away silently and painlessly
- the birth of a child and the death of the mother just hours later
- the painful words, "I want a divorce; I don't love you anymore"
- the sound of gunshots and school children, university students, people gathered for a prayer meeting, and young adults in a night club fall victim to a shooter's bullets

These tragedies and more elicit from us the cry, "We know Job; we are Job." Like him, we suffer and grieve and are left asking, "Why, and why us and those we love?" And, like Job, no one gives us an answer. The author of the book of Job gives his readers an initial answer: God and Satan agreed to let it happen.

Many answers are given to the "why" of our suffering and grief. After Job's children are killed by a strong wind and all of his servants and livestock are stolen or killed, Job's response is one of anguish and grief but not unfaithfulness. Through tears he continues to worship and bless God. And, after a second test agreed to by God and Satan to inflict Job with loathsome sores, Job refuses to explain his suffering by blaming God. He can't explain why he's suffering; he just holds on to his trust in the goodness of God in spite of not understanding the source of his suffering. He grieves in his valley and waits for a word from God.

Job's wife has an explanation for their suffering. She reaches the anger stage of her grief and lashes out at Job and God, saying, "Do you still hold fast your integrity? Curse God, and die" (Job 2:9). Job's wife speaks from her heart and anguish and blames God for their tragedy. She views God as all powerful but unloving.

She's not the only one who attributes tragic losses to an insensitive and uncaring God. I have listened to the anguished voice of Job's wife in church members' responses to their tragic losses. I also have seen some of them come through their grief and reclaim their trust in the goodness of God. We are not told what happened to Job's wife.

The next explanation given to Job's suffering comes from his friends—Eliphaz, Bildad, and Zophar. At first they do a good thing: they sit with Job for a week without saying a word, for they see how distraught their friend is. (A personal request: If tragedy comes to me and you are my friends, please come to see me, but, please, do not stay a whole week! I am not rich and could not provide for you a week's lodging and food. Several hours would be just fine.)

Someone shared with me a story about a mother who sent her 8-year-old son to a store to make a few purchases. She began to worry when he delayed in returning home. When he finally returned she asked him, "What took you so long?" He replied, "On the way home I met Susie who was trying to fix her bicycle." His mother asked, "Why did you do that? You don't know how to fix a bicycle." Her son said, "I know but Susie was crying, and I stayed and helped her cry."

Isn't that what we need when our hearts are breaking? Someone who will not try to fix our broken hearts with theological and psychological explanations, but someone who will sit with us and help us through our valleys of grief.

Job's three friends initially do that, but after a week they break their silence and begin their attempt to explain to Job the meaning of his suffering and grief. He does not need, however, someone trying to convince his head about his brokenness; he needs someone to understand his heart and say, "We'll help you get through this, Job." But Job's three friends cannot conceive of suffering divorced from sin. Job must have done something wrong!

The rest of the book of Job is dialogue between Job, his three friends, and a few others the author weaves into the discussion about human suffering. Job, often depressed and discouraged, holds fast to his belief that God is not punishing him for unconfessed sins. At times he even longs for someone who can stand between him and his accusers and between him and God—"There is no umpire between us, who might lay his hand upon us both" (Job 9:33). Job, even though he knows he is a good person, feels defenseless against a God who answers to no one and Job's friends who accuse him of evil deeds as the cause of his suffering. An umpire might rule in Job's favor, but there isn't one.

Then, with a brilliantly inspired conclusion, the author addresses Job's dilemma—and ours. He invites God to speak from a natural phenomenon: a whirlwind. God speaks first to Job in a series of questions about his use of power in relation to Creation, and about Job's whereabouts when it was happening (Job 38-41): "Were you present when I created all things, Job, and set boundaries for the oceans to be contained?"

On and on God interrogates Job about trying to penetrate the mysteries of Creation with his limited human knowledge. Notice, however, that God does not take Job to task about refusing to interpret his suffering as a result of hidden, unconfessed sins. The only conclusion, then, that makes sense is that God is saying something like this: "Job, you think the world ought to be a place that is always predictable, but it isn't. Things happen that you don't like and neither do I, but it's my world. I made it. It's not perfect. Suffering happens to people like you. And, Job, neither you nor I want it or will it."

Two Jews point us to this kind of interpretation of God's response to Job. Rabbi Harold S. Kushner in his excellent book, *When Bad Things Happen to Good People*, concludes that God is not all powerful but is powerful enough to create a world in which accidents, randomness, and suffering are possible to people as good as Job.[1] The other Jew is Jesus.

One day as Jesus is walking with his disciples, they pass a man blind from birth. According to John 9:2-3, the disciples ask Jesus: "Rabbi, who sinned, this man or his parents, that he was born blind?" Jesus answers, "It was not that this man sinned, or his parents but that the works of God might be made manifest in him."

Jesus' disciples are sharing a belief, prominent in Job's time and in Jesus' day and often in our world today, that all suffering comes from sin. They assume that someone must have sinned for this man to be afflicted with blindness from birth. Jesus makes it clear that there is suffering that has nothing to do with sin, and that God who made this imperfect creation is not on the side of making human suffering and tragedy worse by explaining it as divine punishment. Instead, God is working to help those who suffer. In essence, Jesus says, "Let me show you." He restores the blind man's eyesight and proclaims, "Here is an example of Godness" (my interpretation).

Now, back to Job: After God puts Job in his place, God does a remarkable thing: he comes to Job's defense. He says to Job's three friends, "My wrath is kindled against you, for you have not spoken of me what is right, as my servant Job has" (Job 42:7). Then God requires them to take a burnt offering to Job who will pray for them. He pledges to accept Job's prayer and go easy on his friends. And they do just that.

God's response to Job's suffering and his friends' interpretation of Job's suffering can be instructive to us. When someone is suffering, whether it is you or a friend, don't try to explain it. When we are in the valley of pain, suffering, and grief, we need a shepherding presence that communicates goodness and mercy. That's what Job needed. His friends wanted him to admit his guilt. The Good Shepherd said you are wrong. Job's friends, I assume, believed in the goodness and mercy of God. Apparently, however, to them, God's goodness and mercy were at the service of his judgment, instead of his judgment being at the service of his goodness and mercy.

The book of Job begins with the author presenting an earlier concept of God as one who makes deals with Satan to test people's faith during prearranged and God-approved disasters. The book concludes with the revelation of a God who affirms Job and chastises his friends for misrepresenting his character to Job. He is a God of judgment, but first he is a shepherd—not a capricious God who makes wagers with Satan at the expense of good but not perfect people.

The author ends his story the way we would like all stories to end: "And they lived happily ever after." Job's fame, fortune, and family (another one) are restored. You and I know, however, that many stories of suffering and grief do not end as Job's did. His story of suffering and anguish ended by receiving God's restoring grace. He lost it all and had it all restored with a new family and new stuff.

Grace Emerging from Valleys

As a pastor who has walked with church members into valleys of suffering for more than 50 years, I remember numerous families who came out of their valleys not as Job did with restoring grace. Are they to live on, then, as graceless people? One of my seminary professors gave an appropriate answer to this question: When we don't receive God's restoring grace, we are not left graceless. With grieving faith, we look for God's sustaining grace. Let me illustrate.

In 2001 I became the interim pastor of the First Baptist Church in Whiteville, North Carolina. After our two-year sojourn in Whiteville, a young lady, Sarah Whitson, who had grown up in the church, asked me to officiate her wedding. Pat and I had become friends of her parents, Ron and Barbara Whitson, who were faithful members of the church.

Sarah chose to have her wedding in the Queen's College Chapel in Charlotte, North Carolina, a school associated with many positive memories for Ron and Barbara. Much of their love story happened there while Barbara was a student and Ron was attending nearby Davidson College. The wedding was beautiful and intensified the friendship we already had with the Whitson family.

Fast forward: Several years after the wedding I received a call from Barbara. She said, "Frank, Ron and I are coming to Wilmington. Ron wants to talk to you." (At the time I was minister of pastoral care for the First Baptist Church in Wilmington.) Then she shared with me that Ron had been diagnosed with the dreadful news, "You have terminal cancer."

In our conversation, which took place in the First Baptist Church chapel, Ron said to me, "Frank, I have a concern." I said, "Ron, share whatever you want to; I'm listening." He said, "I just don't feel close to God like I want to."

I wasn't sure what to say. Then I thought of Jesus on the cross and said, "Ron, when Jesus was dying on the cross, he didn't feel God's presence with him. He said, 'My God, why have your abandoned me?' When he said that, Ron, he wasn't pretending; he actually felt forsaken, and yet, at that hour, the Father had never been nearer and was, through his son's suffering, making available enough forgiveness to cover all of the sins of all of the people of all of the ages."

Ron became calm. We finished our visit with prayer. Several days later I received a card from Ron that stated simply: "Thanks, Frank; I'm ready for my transition."

After my visit with Ron I thought to myself: It doesn't seem fair. Then I remembered what John Claypool, our former pastor at Crescent Hill Baptist Church in Louisville, Kentucky, shared about Dr. Reuel Howe, a leader in the field of pastoral psychology.

In a visit Reuel had with a friend who had a terminal illness, he said "Bob, it doesn't seem fair." Bob responded, "It's OK, Reuel; I've come to accept death as an old friend in a new garb." Dr. Howe then asked, "Could you say more about that? I'm not sure I understand." Bob replied:

> Reuel, all my life I've been experiencing exits that turned out to be entrances. The day I started to school I got up and was ready to play with my familiar things in the backyard. But Mom said, "Bob, you're going to put on different clothes today; you're going to school." Reuel, I didn't want to go to school. I wanted to stay in my little, familiar world. But I had to leave those things, and that exit was an entrance to a new world—teachers, friends, and learning. And it was the same way when I left elementary school for high school and high school for college: each exit became an entrance to a new world. One day I was at home and looked out at where I played as a young child and thought about all I would have missed if I had just stayed at home. And, Reuel, I believe death is one more of God's exits that becomes an entrance into a new stage of life.

Dr. Howe congratulated his friend for his insight and ended their visit with prayer.

About two weeks later Bob's wife called, "Reuel, Bob died and we want you to speak at his funeral." Dr. Howe honored that request. As the service ended and he and the other minister were leading the casket and family toward the narthex of the church, he looked up and saw above the door the letters, **EXIT**. At that moment he remembered Bob's words: With God, every exit is an entrance.

I shared Dr. Howe's story at Ron Whitson's funeral. Bob's family and Ron's family did not receive the kind of restoring grace that Job did. Were they left graceless? Not at all! They received God's sustaining grace in the belief that beyond death, life and love and relationships go on in some form of blessed and recognizable continuity. Is the exit part painful? Yes, it is! It was painful for Bob's family and Barbara Whitson and her family—and for my Aunt Sally.

Aunt Sally's daughter, Lillian, died when she was 33 years old. The doctor said she had a heart murmur. She left a husband, Lee Burgess, and three children: Shirley, 12; Sonny, 8; and Donnie, 6. Back in the 1940s, most funerals were held in church sanctuaries. We gathered for Lillian's funeral in the sanctuary of Northside Baptist Church in Rock Hill, South Carolina. Lillian's family was seated front and center. Rev. J. J. Boone delivered the eulogy. Mr. L. F. Crocker, a mill worker and volunteer choir director, led the choir.

At the end of the service when the choir sang, "Amazing Grace," Aunt Sally could not contain her feelings. She cried, raised her arm, and said, "Praise God!" I was puzzled as an 11-year-old boy. Her daughter was dead. Lillian was one of the nicest, most loving persons I had ever known, and her mother was praising God at her funeral.

Much later, in my 30s, I came to realize what Aunt Sally's praise meant. She was not praising God for Lillian's death. She was celebrating because she believed there was a God to whom she could commit her daughter for safekeeping until they were united again. Her praise was the praise of Bob's family, of Barbara Whitson and her family, and of all of us who lose for a while those we love. In our valleys of grief the "Great Thou Art" gives us God's sustaining grace.

Note

[1] Harold S. Kushner, *When Bad Things Happen to Good People* (New York: Avon Books, 1981), 113-31.

PART TWO
Categories of Grief

. . . a man of sorrows, and acquainted with grief
—*Isaiah 53:3*

Before we leave our focus on horizontal or temporal grief and move to a consideration of transcendent or vertical grief, I want to share with you some pastoral data related to the different categories of grief. To care effectively for grieving people, ministers and counselors need to be aware of the nature and intensity of the grief of those to whom they minister. And, of course, they must be open to being helped to resolve their own grief experiences as they help church members and counselees with theirs.

From years of pastoral experience and from teachers and colleagues in the department of pastoral psychology of the Southern Baptist Theological Seminary in the early 1970s—and especially from Dr. Wayne E. Oates' lectures and his excellent book, *Your Particular Grief*—I learned about five types of grief:

1. anticipatory grief
2. delayed grief
3. prolonged grief
4. distorted grief
5. pathological grief

Anticipatory Grief

Some of our grief happens before the actual loss takes place. A doctor may say, "I have your test results and I wish I could give you good news, but . . ." Then he proceeds to tell you that you have pancreatic, lung, or colon cancer. At that point fear, anxiety, and dread may become anticipatory grief for the patient and her family.

I have been the pastor of some people, not many, who, after experiencing significant losses, tend to refocus their lives away from present living toward an anticipated dark future. Then, consciously or unconsciously, they may try to keep that future at bay. This form of anticipatory grief may rob children, teenagers, and adults from having good, fuller lives in the present and the future. Jesus counsels us in Matthew 6:24 to live courageously and fully—not one future at a time, but one day at a time.

People, of course, are different, and in their differentness respond in various ways to life and to the aging process and to death itself. Some may go through stages of response while others may clutch to denial until aging runs its course and death comes. I have been the pastor of those who have remained very quiet through the process of dying, while others have talked, cried, and spoken of what they believe they see on the other side of death. Basically, people experience dying and death in a variety of ways according to their unique natures. Let me illustrate what I mean by sharing the stories of two couples from my days as a pastor.

When I became pastor of the First Baptist Church of Kingsport, Tennessee in 1980, Mary Frances Gregory was the church organist. For Sunday worship services she accompanied William Robinson, the minister of music, as he led the chancel choir and the congregation in singing sacred music. Mary Frances was married to L. P. Gregory, who had grown up on a farm in southwest Virginia.

As a young man, he moved to Kingsport (about 70 miles from his birthplace) and after several jobs, opened a hardware store that supported well his wife and children. Then, not content with his level of success, L. P., in his 50s, made a bold move and decided to enter the insurance business.

Once when he and I were talking about his job he said, "When I decided to be an insurance man, I knew I wanted to get all of the training necessary to do it right."

That is exactly what L. P. did. He learned his trade well enough to win the trust of coal companies in bordering states north of Tennessee. He sold to them corporate insurance policies that helped L. P. become very successful in his new professional endeavor.

Then one day my secretary called and said, "L. P. Gregory is here and wants to see you." I thought he probably wanted to invite me to play golf. When he entered my office, however, I knew it wasn't golf he had on his mind. He sat down, breathed heavily, and said, "Frank, Mary Frances has been diagnosed with cervical cancer." (Mary Frances had already retired as church organist, and she and L. P. had enjoyed a number of good years traveling and sharing time with their family and friends.)

After that day in my office I began doing what pastors do: I visited Mary Frances in her home, and, as her health deteriorated, I visited her in the hospital. Mary Frances died in 1992. I delivered the eulogy at her funeral in the sanctuary where she had served faithfully as church organist for many years.

L. P. and his family did a lot of their grieving before Mary Frances died. I was not surprised, then, when about a year after her death L. P. shared with me that he had begun dating Keith Hamilton.

During the long months of anticipatory grief Mary Frances and L. P. chose to be practical as they looked toward the possibility of different futures. One day, as they talked, Mary Frances said, "L. P., if and when I die, I don't want you to live alone." L. P., I'm sure, thanked her and asked (in jest) if she had anyone in mind for him. She answered (according to L. P.), "Yes, I do." She mentioned Keith Hamilton, who had lost her husband, Red, years earlier. Keith had a beautiful soprano voice and sang many inspirational solos as a member of the sanctuary choir. She and Mary Frances had been good friends for years.

L. P., following his deceased wife's counsel, began a romantic relationship with Keith that led to a marriage. Their wedding took place in our new church chapel. I remember saying to myself, as I planned to officiate their wedding ceremony, "It's L. P. and Keith—not Mary Frances." Guess what? When we came to the vows I said, "Do you, L. P., take Mary Frances (pause) Keith?" L. P. and Keith and their family members smiled and then laughed. They were so kind and forgiving. Keith said later, "You figured out a way to include Mary Frances in the ceremony." Not really: Mary Frances had already done that in helping L. P. to choose his second bride as a practical and realistic part of their anticipatory grief.

In my imagination I can see Mary Frances and Red giving each other "celestial high fives" in affirmation to their former spouses' earthly joy. L. P. and Keith had a happy marriage for many years.

One Sunday in 1980 when I was pastor of the First Baptist Church in Statesboro, Georgia, I mentioned in my sermon that Pat and I had grown up in Rock Hill, South Carolina. After the service, as I spoke to exiting worshippers, P. J. and Lorene Burns, two visitors, shared with me that they, too, were from South Carolina. In the fall of that year I became the Burns' pastor when I accepted the call of the First Baptist Church in Kingsport, Tennessee. Mrs. Burns was a member of the church's pastor search committee and the committee's first contact with me as a potential pastor.

In addition to being their pastor, Pat and I became good friends with the Burns. We have many happy memories of being guests in their lovely home and at the country club's bountiful table. These memories made more intense our sadness when Lorene began showing signs of Alzheimer's disease. P. J., who had retired from a management position with the Tennessee Eastman Chemical Plant and had become involved in real estate projects, was very attentive to Lorene as her mind, body, and personality were assaulted by her degenerative disease. Trips to the hospital and absences from church attendance became more frequent. P. J. and his family were facing a different kind of anticipatory grief—not the anticipation of Lorene's physical death, but rather the slow demise of her mind's ability to function properly.

The day came when P. J. shared with me their plans to move to Durham, North Carolina. He had researched and found a facility there that specialized in the care of persons like Lorene, with living quarters for spouses and family caretakers too. The move, however, was a painful decision for P. J. and his family. Although the Burns had children and family members who lived in and around Durham, Kingsport and our church were home and extended family to them. We grieved with them as they watched a kind of death in slow motion to a beloved mother and wife.

The last time Pat and I saw P. J. and Lorene was at their place in Durham when I was participating in a mini-sabbatical at Duke Divinity School. Pat had driven from Kingsport and after having lunch with P. J. in a home-atmosphere restaurant in Hillsborough, North Carolina, we visited Lorene in the reception room of her facility—a beautiful place! The visit was like old times for a while. Lorene smiled and even laughed some, but then she retreated inward, which was P. J.'s signal to take her back to her room. Next, P. J. took us to his place, an apartment separate from but very close to Lorene's room. He could look from his window and see Lorene's window below.

P. J. had transformed his anticipatory grief into an occasion to make caring and realistic plans for Lorene and himself, but he did more. He joined a support group, sponsored by Duke Hospital, for spouses and family members with people like Lorene. He has even served as the representative of the group in a nationally televised program about how to live courageously and caringly when unexpected and unwanted diseases such as Alzheimer's comes to someone's family.

Delayed Grief

In 1971 I became the pastor of Melbourne Heights Baptist Church in Louisville, Kentucky. At the same time I was working on a master's degree in pastoral care at Southern Seminary, located about three miles from the church. I chose as the topic for my thesis, "Forgiveness as a Factor in the Management of Guilt in Parents of Mentally Retarded Children." (Today, we would use a more appropriate and caring term instead of mental retardation: "intellectually disabled.")

In order to give me a role in the lives of families with this particular challenge, my seminary supervisor, Dr. John Boyle, arranged for me to serve as chaplain in a diagnostic center for intellectually disabled children. Parents brought their children there for diagnosis and counsel from a team of professional people including medical doctors, psychologists, social workers, and others. I was a part of that team approach. Along with seeing the other team members, the parents met with me. During my time at the center I counseled with 22 couples. They shared with me their feelings about having children who were different. Their basic and most pervasive feeling was grief.

I recall a conversation I had with Jerry and Bobbie Baker, the parents of a 3-year-old Down syndrome son, Roger, whom they brought to the center for evaluation and counsel:

Chaplain: Come in. My name is Frank Hawkins, and I believe you are Jerry and Bobbie Baker. Is that right?
Jerry: That's right. We brought our son, Roger, for evaluation. (They seemed tense but were very polite).
Chaplain: How old is Roger now?
Bobbie: He's three. Had his third birthday in July.
Chaplain: Do you have other children?
Bobbie: No, he's our only child. We can give him all of our attention and love. I told Jerry the other day that we'll be able to have him with us when other kids are up and gone. (Bobbie was smiling, but it was a tense smile. Jerry was rubbing his right arm with his left hand).

Jerry: That's right.

Chaplain: I know you love Roger a great deal. Bringing him to this center is an act of your love. And, I do appreciate your sharing with me your positive feelings about Roger. But, if you have negative feelings about his condition, that's OK, too. (Jerry and Bobbie seemed to relax. They began to share with me feelings of hurt about Roger's disability).

Jerry: When Roger was born, we could not believe it. We had expected him to be like other kids. It hurt a lot.

Bobbie: I cried for a whole month after Roger was born. I loved him, but I was hurt for him and us.

Chaplain: What do you do with these kinds of feelings? Do you have anyone or a group to share them with?

Jerry: We just keep them to ourselves and in the family.

Chaplain: Would you be interested in meeting with a group of parents who also have Down syndrome children?

Jerry: Yes, we would! Where do they meet?

I shared with Jerry and Bobbie the details about a parents' support group that met on a weekly basis. They accepted the invitation to join the group. As they left my office, I noticed a changed attitude and a sense of hope in both parents. I let them know that both their positive and negative feelings about Roger were acceptable to me and to the Good Shepherd whom I represented. I believe they got the message. Through their support group they would not be alone. They would be able to cry and laugh, express frustrations and anger, and find community for themselves and their child.

All of the couples I counseled at the diagnostic center described to me a kind of grieving process they were experiencing after discovering their children were intellectually disabled. All of them had gone through the first stage of shock and numbness. Some were still experiencing the emotional stage of crying and questioning: Why us and our children? Some were angry with each other and with God. A few couples felt guilty and mentioned premarital sex and poor church attendance as possible reasons for divine punishment. Several couples were still in denial and hoping for a cure that would make their children whole again. Some of the couples were getting close to the reality stage: accepting the loss of the expected children and embracing their real children.

Affirming and supporting parents and families who, simultaneously, encounter the loss of the expected child and the acceptance of the real child is an area of our humanity that still needs creative attention. Grieving doesn't quite fit in with the birth of a child. Therefore, parents of intellectually disabled children, who do feel a sense of loss, tend to do their grieving in private. Their grief, then, may be delayed and interfere with the acceptance of the real child. And, the whisper of the tempter in Genesis 3:5, "You will be like God," may hinder the acceptance of imperfection in birth and life.

In the adventure of living, any time when we can accept nothing less than perfection in ourselves and others, perfection may become an enemy to the release of realistic potentials. Hope, according to Father William Lynch in his book *Images of Hope*, is always rooted in the acceptance of reality. When we can accept our real selves and the same in others, including our offspring, real hope is born. Consider the following example.

Ben and Amy Wright and their four children—Lillie, 17; Emma Grace, 16; Beau, 12; and Bitty, 6—are members of our church in Wilmington, North Carolina. Beau and Bitty are intellectually disabled. Amy shared in a *Wilmington Star News* article (June 16, 2016) that she and Ben are embarrassed now about the scary feelings they had when they learned Beau had a genetic disorder typically associated with physical and intellectual growth delays. Then six years later Bitty was born with Down syndrome.

But after living through the early stages of grief, fear, and hurt, Ben and Amy made a courageous decision: they would embrace their four children and challenge them to accept their individual potentials. For Amy, with Ben's approval and support, that has become a vocation (a calling) to encourage their children, especially Beau and Bitty, to reach for what is achievable and possible as Down syndrome persons.

That calling reached a moment of divine inspiration one morning in 2015. While taking a shower (when Amy says she does her best thinking), she visualized a Beau's Coffee Shop that would employ people with a range of disabilities including Down syndrome, cerebral palsy, autism, and others. Beau's Coffee opened in February 2016 at the corner of Wrightsville and Kerr avenues in Wilmington. It had 19 employees (more than 100 job applications have been received), and Amy planned to double that number.

She soon relocated Beau's Coffee—renaming it Bitty and Beau's Coffee—to a 5,000-square foot facility on New Centre Drive that accommodates more jobs and a greater variety of menu offerings, thanks to Rippy Automobiles Inc. that provides a rent-free building on its business campus.

In March 2017, Amy and Beau's employees "skyped" into the *Rachael Ray Show*. Ray blessed her guests and shared a hope for Beau's Coffee: "A Beau's Coffee Shop on every corner coast to coast." Amy also wants to see a Beau's in cities across America. In fact, at the end of 2017, Beau's Coffee will offer franchising opportunities. Owners will have a choice between operating as a for-profit or non-profit business. The selection process, however, will carefully present an unchanging expectation: owners have to be more passionate about the social profit than the financial gain. Amy's dream and goal is to reduce significantly the percent of intellectually disabled persons' unemployment (90 percent) by offering them the dignity and joy of earning a respectable salary for honest work.

It seems that Amy and Ben have taken their embarrassment over feelings of fear, hurt, and grief and transformed them into a place of hope for Beau, Bitty, and many other intellectually disabled persons in Wilmington, and potentially, nationwide. (In the fall of 2017 Amy and Ben Wright will open a new Bitty and Beau's in Charleston, South Carolina.) What an example for us all!

Prolonged Grief

One day while I was pastor of Melbourne Heights Baptist Church, Alice Combs came to see me after we had celebrated communion. She said, "Pastor, is there anything we can do to make communion more meaningful? We do it the same way every time, and it seems so dull. It's too important to be that way."

I was irritated for a while. Then I thought: she may be right. I talked it over with the church staff, and we decided to have our next communion service at night in the fellowship hall—something entirely new for the church and me.

We put candles on the tables and placed the elements at the head of each table where a deacon would sit and serve family-style. The youth choir sang inspirational music, and I gave a brief devotional titled "Come to the Table." I spoke of how all of us have tables to which we have been invited—in our childhood and youth—and tables to which we have invited others—our children, family, and friends. I then explained how Jesus continues the family motif by inviting us to our Father's table that he prepares with his own blood and body.

After the devotional and prayer, with soft background music playing, the deacons began the table communion conversation as the elements were shared from person to person. The fellowship hall became a sanctuary. For the first time in my life one of my children shared with me the bread and the cup. I had never shared this sacred meal with Pat individually. That night, however, I served Pat and said, "Pat, I am honored to share with you this bread and cup as our Lord commanded us to do. I love you."

As we communed around the tables, we heard someone crying. We thought, these must be tears of joy. When the service was over we found out what happened. The tears belonged to one of our young single women.

About a year prior to that evening, she was driving to a wedding rehearsal; her mother was with her. Paula lost control of the car, and there was a tragic single-car accident. She was hospitalized for weeks with multiple injuries. Her mother died. Paula was so traumatized by the tragedy that her conscious mind could not grieve or admit what had happened. She had remained in a state of unresolved, prolonged grief—until that night.

The Lord's table became Paula's safe place to own and share her grief. She began to talk about her mother, and as the tears flowed freely, the inner healing she needed was mediated through communion and caring friends gathered at our Lord's table of grace and forgiveness.

Distorted Grief

Jim, in his 70s, was a faithful member of Harmony Baptist Church, located about 17 miles from Rock Hill, South Carolina. I became the pastor of that rural, antebellum church in 1960. In one of my first sermons to the congregation I announced my intention to make "let's get acquainted" visits in the homes of our members. Church members received the idea well.

When I arrived at Jim's house (a wood-framed, early 1900s structure surrounded by majestic oak trees), Jim and his wife, Joan, greeted me warmly. They led me across their home's wide front porch and through a long hall that gave access to various rooms with antique furnishings bequeathed to Jim by his parents who died in the 1940s.

We sat in their family room and talked about our church, community, and the historical link they had with the cotton industry, from the days of slave labor to the present. Although they missed some of the glory of the Old South, they realized—as the book *Gone with the Wind* portrayed it—those days were gone forever.

As we talked, I noticed that Jim kept looking at a non-functioning Seth Thomas pendulum clock sitting on a wood mantle over a stone fireplace. Evidently, Joan noticed his frequent looks at the clock and excused herself to check on some items being prepared on the kitchen stove.

With Joan absent, Jim looked at me and said, "I guess you wonder why the clock is not telling time." I responded, "Well, I did notice you looking at the clock and wondered if it was broken or just needed rewinding." After a pause, Jim smiled and said, "No, it's not broken; but I don't intend to ever rewind it." I thought to myself, "There's got to be a story here." Then Jim said, "You see, pastor, the clock is stopped at 4:35. That's the time my mother died back in the '40s in this very room. In that moment I stopped the clock and decided it would always remind me of the day, hour, and minute when she passed."

As a young pastor, I wasn't sure what to say. I'm sure I tried to support Jim as he reflected on his mother's death, a decade and a half in the past. I'm not sure, however, if Jim's grief qualifies as distorted or not. Maybe it does. Maybe the stopped clock, in the very room where his mother died, became a kind of shrine that ushered Jim into a place of timeless fantasy, where mystically and emotionally mother and child were joined again.

Fantasy or not, this I know: Jim and Joan were faithful members of our church and active members of the larger community to which they belonged. The non-functioning clock on the mantle helped to keep alive memories of his mother. Whatever degree of fantasy that might have included did not isolate them from the real world where responsibility and mutuality are essential to sustain relationships.

All of us probably have some degree of fantasizing in our lives and relationships. Real distortion comes, however, when fantasy takes over and becomes an escape from real life.

Distorted grief can come from losses of human life where bodies of loved ones are never found. On July 23, 2016, for example, the *Wilmington Star News* published an article about a Boeing 777 that vanished in a flight from Kuala Lumpur, Malaysia to Beijing, China on March 8, 2014. The article by Eileen Ng, writing for the Associated Press, shared that after an extensive search effort costing approximately $135 million, Malaysia, Australia, and China had decided to suspend the search at the conclusion of the current search of 46,300 square miles of the Indian Ocean. If this last effort to find Malaysia Airlines Flight 370 proved unsuccessful, the plane and its 239 passengers may never be found.

The article referred to the plane's disappearance as "aviation's greatest mystery," although the Malaysian government has concluded that it was deliberately steered off course. If the mystery is never solved, those who grieve may experience unresolved grief that could lead to fantasy and distortion.

When people face such debilitating unresolved grief, caring pastors, church members, family members, and friends would do well to guide them toward competent and caring professional help. They need and deserve it.

Pathological Grief

As a pastor, I enjoyed visiting homebound members. Because people are living longer, churches now have more members in their 80s and 90s. Retirement communities have evolved into campus-like institutions that provide different levels of care: independent living, assisted living, personal care, memory care, and hospice care.

In reflecting back on my 55 years of ministry, however, my interaction with senior adults indicates a resounding conclusion: They prefer to live in their own homes as long as possible, with assistance from their children (if they have children). Many churches, especially larger ones, have added senior adult ministers to address this growing need—not to supplant, but to supplement their family's primary roles of support and care.

This was the case for Ethel Graham, 78, a member of Melbourne Heights Baptist Church when I became her pastor in 1971. Ethel had three children: two sons who lived in other cities and a daughter who lived nearby in Louisville. In reasonably good health, Ethel was able to live at home with minimal help from her daughter and weekly telephone calls and occasional visits from her sons. Ethel and I became friends during my frequent visits in her home. It wasn't exactly like a "mother and son friendship," but it was close to that. We laughed, joked, gossiped a little, and shared feelings of sadness about other church members as we prayed together.

Then, out of the blue, sadness came to Ethel. Her older son, in his mid-50s, died. Ethel's heart was broken. She attended the funeral and returned home and continued to grieve heavily for weeks. Parental grief presents a special kind of bereavement, even when the child is almost a senior adult. Then, it happened again. Just months after her older son's death, her younger son died.

I'll never forget my visit with Ethel the day her daughter shared with me the bad news. I immediately went to Ethel's home. When I entered the front door, Ethel was sitting on her sofa—motionless. At first she did not recognize my presence. Her face read like a mini-dictionary on sorrow: pale, empty, bereft, abandoned, listless, spiritless, Job-like. I said, "Ethel." There was no response. When she spoke, she did not look at me—didn't call my name. She spoke seven words: "Don't say anything. It hurts too bad." In that moment I remembered Job and his friends, who sat with him in silence a whole week after his devastating losses. I honored Ethel's request. I sat down by her side and shared her silence with her.

I was not a psychologist or psychiatrist, but as a Christian pastor and counselor, I knew Ethel would need professional help to return from the deep waters that some call "pathological grief."

Ethel's daughter, Betty, and I agreed that her mother's grief was diseased enough to require professional counseling. I was pleased with that decision for a good and practical reason: I had received and accepted a call as pastor of the First Baptist Church in Statesboro, Georgia. We were a family in transition with our house in Louisville sold, our furniture being loaded for shipping, and a church waiting to receive a new pastor and his family. And I knew, without any doubt, that Ethel's church family and ministerial staff would continue to support her during her walk through the valley of sorrow.

About a year later I received a card from Betty. She wanted me to know that Ethel was responding well to her counseling and that her mother had a message for me: "You'll never know how much your visit and presence meant to me on that awful day." It made me realize that when people are hurting, the thing they remember more than our words is our presence.

Isn't that true also when we celebrate our Lord's presence at the communion table? In his physical absence we remember his presence for us in the garden of Gethsemane, on the cross, and in his resurrection. And as we remember, he is with us mystically and wonderfully as host of the sacramental meal.

PART THREE
Vertical Grief

*I will turn their mourning into joy. I will comfort them,
and give them gladness for sorrow.*
—*Jeremiah 31:13*

Earlier we explored the horizontal dimension of grief. We turn now to the vertical dimension. In both of these we live in relationships where loss and grief occur. The horizontal relationship is both interpersonal (between us and other humans) and intrapersonal (between us and ourselves—having to do with self-worth, self-concept, and self-awareness).

The vertical relationship is also interpersonal. It exists between us and the Transcendent One. In the language of faith and religion, it is the relationship between God the Creator and humans created in the image of God. In the language of philosophy, it is the relationship between the Source or First Cause that is responsible for our being alive. I choose to believe the Source is personal and interpersonal and creates us to live in relationships with him and other humans.

In other words, we are not complete persons in isolation. In the Creation account, God makes this very clear: "It is not good that the man should be alone" (Gen. 2:18). This judgment came before the fall—before the relationship between God and humanity was broken. What was not good before the fall, when the image of God was still intact? It was humanity without relationships! And if this is true for humanity, it must be true for God, in whose image we are made. If God had remained isolated and self-contained, the Source of all things could be defined as being narcissistic.

Creation, then, is a declaration from God: "I am relational and choose to create relational persons who will be defined not in isolation but in relationships with one another—marriage, children, community, and society—and with me, their Source." Therefore, our identity and definition exist in our selfhood but also include our horizontal and vertical relationships.

We have seen in the first part of this book that when we suffer losses in our horizontal relationships, we experience grief. We lose a part of our selves when we lose persons we love in marriage, parenting, family, and friendship. This is no less true in the transcendent or vertical relationship that is also a part of who God is and who we are as persons created in God's image.

Because God creates what he loves and we exist in his image with the capacity to love and be loved, it follows that when the vertical relationship is broken or lost, grief comes to God and us—just as it does in our human relationships. It's not that God grieves because we do; rather, we grieve because God does, and, in his image, we do also. As 1 John 4:19 tells us, "We love because he first loved us." So, we grieve because God first grieves for us.

The Bible, therefore, is a book about a loving God who creates persons in his own image who are free to make real choices. And when we make choices that harm or damage our relationship with him, it brings grief to both God and us. And what does God do with his grief? God moves with purpose through history to reclaim what he has lost.

Grief and the Image of God

I am attempting to bring together two dimensions of grief, horizontal and vertical, by employing a term that connects both dimensions: "the image of God." I understand this biblical term as an inclusive and exclusive declaration that places humanity in Creation. This means we are not co-equal and co-eternal with the Creator. We are here by someone's design and purposes—not our own. This gives us a kinship with the limits and potentials of all things created.

The term, however, has an inclusive meaning. The Creator bestows on us the gift of likeness and similarity. We are to collaborate with God in the care and cultivation of Creation while being ourselves a part of it. Genesis 1 tells this story of Creation and God's gift and commission to humanity.

But how are we like the Creator? Where do we see this image of God? Do we see it in the Old Testament? Do we see it in other religions? Do we see it in nature? Do we see it in other people and ourselves?

We see the image of God in all of these places, but we see it imperfectly. The original image of God has become marred and disfigured in the course of human history. And, as the apostle Paul states, "We see in a mirror dimly" (1 Cor. 17:12), which renders our knowledge, prophecy, and relationships imperfect.

Where do we see the imperfect image of God restored to its original fullness and undimmed meaning? Not in another mirror that can only reflect another imperfect image of what we have lost, but in a person who reveals in human form the essence of who God is and the essence of who we were intended to be.

In John 14:8, Philip the disciple seeks the answers we seek when he says, "Lord, show us the Father and we shall be satisfied." Jesus responds, "He who has seen me has seen the Father." Philip and the other disciples know that Jesus is human. They have fished with him, eaten with him, laughed and cried with him, argued with him, and followed him. He is a man, a human as good as the womb can produce. The disciples know, however, that Jesus is more.

The early Christian community and church leaders would affirm Jesus' answer to Philip: Jesus is the God man, in whom the fullness of God and the fullness of humanness co-exist. In other words, in his being God in the flesh, Jesus reveals to us the essence of who God is—not in terms of quantity but of quality (God did not vacate eternity during Jesus' time on the earth). In his being human, Jesus reveals to us the essence of what it means to be human with the image of God fully restored.

Let's look now at the essential nature and characteristics of God and humanness revealed in Jesus as defined by faith, hope, and love in action.

Faith, Hope, and Love as Relational Virtues

Paul in the "Love Chapter," 1 Corinthians 13, makes an assertion about these three relational virtues: "So faith, hope, love abide, these three; but the greatest of these is love" (v. 13). There are three truths about Paul's statement that are palpable.

First, these virtues belong to the eternal order—they abide. Second, they exist in relationships—not in isolation. Love that is self-contained is not based on self-worth and self-acceptance but on self-rejection, forever seeking to validate itself by using other people. Third, of the three, love is the greatest. All three relational virtues belong to the eternal order, but love stands above faith and hope. Why?

Let me attempt to give relational definitions for faith, hope, and love as an imperfect answer to the "Why" I raised.

Faith

Paul first mentions faith, the abiding virtue that releases powers among people to achieve positive good. Show me a marriage, family, church, school, or other institution where healthy faith is alive, and I will show you communication where creative powers are being released among persons for the achieving of positive good. But when faith is lost or deteriorates into unbelief, those creative powers are shut down and may be changed into negative powers.

This happened to Jesus when he returned to Nazareth during his ministerial career. Instead of finding faith there, he found unbelief and could not do any mighty works (Mark 8:5-6). Powers existed in Jesus to achieve positive good, but a lack of faith negated them.

Hope

Next, Paul recognizes hope, the enduring relational virtue that releases the power of the future for the achieving of positive good. One of the best books I've read about hope is *Images of Hope* in which William F. Lynch locates the power of hope in the human faculty of imagination. He writes about hope as the ability to imagine the possible. That ability cannot function alone or in isolation; it needs community to move from imagination to realization of dreams. A part of that movement, according to Dr. Lynch, is keeping what is hopeful separated from what is hopeless.[1]

For example, I used to be a good softball pitcher. If I were to offer, however, my services to the Atlanta Braves as a solution to their pitching problems, that would not be hopeful. Hope begins in the power to imagine, but is rooted in reality. Some people, unfortunately, invest their hope ability in what is hopeless, or unreal, and miss their own futures. This does not mean that hope does not require courage. Often what is truly hopeful faces discouraging challenges and at first may seem hopeless. Faith, indeed, is needed for hope to persevere.

Love

Paul concludes with love, the abiding, relational virtue that releases powers among persons to achieve positive good in the present. We cannot love in the past; it's gone. We cannot love in the future, but we can plan to love in the future (that's called hope). The only time for love's realization is in the "now"—the present. All three virtues, then, converge in present time. Love takes faith with one hand and hope with the other and releases the power of all three in concrete actions of positive good in the dynamic present.

That, I believe, is why Paul calls love the greatest of the three. Love is where faith and hope find their channel of expression as practical, positive good. As James 2:17 tells us, "Faith by itself, if it has no works, is dead." So is hope. But as a trinity, focused toward action in present time, they are conveyers of the queen of virtues—the grace of God that makes faith, hope, and love possible in our human connections.

From my theological education and many years of ministering to people, I have come to this conclusion: In 1 Corinthians, Paul is holding up a mirror (not like the one he mentioned that is dim and distorted) in which we see the image of God restored in Jesus. God's essential nature, then, is this: At God's core are gracious faith, hope, and love in action, with love as the cohesive center. As 1 John 4:16 states, it is God's essential definition: "So we know and believe the love God has for us. God is love, and he who abides in love abides in God, and God abides in him."

Consider this explanation about the virtues of God present in terms of two concentric circles: In the center of the first circle, place the words faith, hope, and love, with love at the exact center. These virtues define God, with love as the greatest of the three.

In the second circle, place the various characteristics of God: holiness, righteousness, goodness, anger, all-wise, creative, all-powerful, purposeful, eternal, sovereign, spirit, all-present, judge, just, and so on. These characteristics also define God but are at the service of the virtues placed in the first circle—faith, hope, and love—but ultimately at the service of love that is the integrating center of who God is. For example, God does get angry and judge human behavior, but his anger and judgments never replace love that occupies the center of who God is. (I learned this view of God's anger from James E. Tull, my seminary professor of systematic theology in 1959, who said "God's anger is his rejection of our rejection of him.")

In other words, love will not let us go without a fight. This means that all of God's other characteristics are at the service of God's love. They are themselves expressions of who God is at his core—love! Therefore, whatever God is doing—creating, judging, expressing anger, punishing, demonstrating power, imparting justice and goodness—is God's eternal love in action.

Where do we see this image of God? In ourselves? In others? In religion? In the Old Testament? The apostle Paul, who thought he saw it in the Old Testament, concluded that in all of these places we catch glimpses of the image of God, but that it is only in a living and breathing person, Jesus, that we see the image of who God is and the image of what is missing in us.

Jesus and the Resolution of Grief

Let's now examine what is missing, or better still, what we have lost and why we are grieving—both God and us. Continuing to employ the image of concentric circles, consider the modern human picture. What do we see in the inner circle? Love buttressed by faith and hope? Love employing power, creativity, wisdom, and purpose to reach just and unselfish goals?

This type of love is present in human lives—in some more than others—but our love and the love of others can be replaced by anger and other characteristics, and become either neutralized or rendered destructive for periods of time. Love and its companions, faith and hope, may be compromised and banished by greed and selfishness and make of us conflicted souls in the center where love is our only true definition.

Is there anything or anyone who can say to us these words? "You are grieving, world, because you have lost the image of what it means to be human? You are grieving over the loss of your vital connection to your vertical selfhood, and the one who created you is grieving, too, and rejects your rejection of him. And, the reason he rejects you is this: God loves you with an everlasting love and will not let you go without a fight."

Jesus is that divine and human voice that says: "Look at me. I have come with a message from God. He loves you, grieves for you, and waits for you to return to him and to your true selves as persons created in God's image. And I am going to be before your eyes a living example of the image of God that you have lost, and I will be the divine-human bridge across which you can return home to God and to your true selves as my siblings and God's daughters and sons."

This is why I write about vertical grief. Writing only about horizontal or temporal grief would be insensitive to a grief process that is both relational and existential. In horizontal grief we mourn the loss of relationships (of persons and things) that are timed and exist within the boundaries of birth and death. These losses do not threaten our existence (or should not). In vertical grief we mourn the loss of relationship with the one who created us and sustains our very existence.

Søren Kierkegaard, a Danish theologian of the 1800s, gives us perspective about this difference. Based on the words of Ecclesiastes 3:1, "To everything there is a season . . .," he argues in his book, *Purity of Heart*, that God cannot be placed within time limits. God creates time and places all things finite in time, but God is timeless.[2]

Our world, in general, is grieving a vertical loss as though it were a horizontal one. We know how the process of grieving a temporal loss is supposed to end—in the acceptance of the loss. Failing to accept it would be relating to the loss as if it were an existential loss without which we can no longer survive and thrive. In both grief dimensions there are similarities. A grieving person experiences shock, numbness, emotional release, guilt, anger, and denial. The final stages of grief, however, are quite different. In horizontal grief the process ends with accepting the loss. In vertical grief the process ends not as acceptance of the loss but as, hopefully, the restoration of what has been lost.

I repeat: our world is trying to end its vertical grief as a horizontal one. We are behaving as though we can get over our loss of God and move on to create our lives in our own finite images. In the words of Dr. Pope Duncan, "We are losing our sense of transcendence." And, when we no longer look upward, we create horizontal gods in our distorted human images that become denials of our true selves. When we deny, then, our true selves as persons created in the image of God, our true selves mourn the loss and our false selves create the illusion of joy to cover up the denial of our true identity. This, I believe, is a source of self-rejection and inner conflict that helps to explain much of the hate, violence, and abuse in our world community.

When we lose our self-definition as being the children of God, it follows that we will also lose our relational definition as brothers and sisters of others who are fellow humans. With no God above us who creates and loves us all, we are free to create a convenient god in our own image, with our own societal and religious preferences. God, no doubt, grieves over this and rejects our rejection of him as the lover of all he has created.

The Bible, then, is a story about a loving God who creates persons who are free to choose between good and evil. It asserts that in the beginning and through the ages we have listened to the voices of evil, "You shall be as gods" (Gen. 3:5). In other words, we can create our own identity as our own deity. God grieves over our choice, as evidenced in both the Old and New Testaments.

In the book of Isaiah, the divine presence in human form is "a man of sorrows, and acquainted with grief" (53:3), and "surely he has borne our griefs and carried our sorrows" (53:4). In the New Testament, Jesus laments: "O Jerusalem, Jerusalem, killing the prophets and stoning those who are sent to you! How often would I have gathered your children together as a hen gathers her brood under her wings, and you would not!" (Luke 13:34).

But God, who is defined as sheer love, will not end his grief by accepting what he has lost. God refuses to say, "Go on your way of denial and destruction. Why should I care?" No! Faith believes! Hope sees all that God creates belonging to his future. And love—the core of God's being—never fails. God, then, enters history to end his grief and ours, not in cutting his losses by cutting us loose from him, but by restoring Creation to his original intent. Paul captures the essence of this intent when he wrote, "In Christ, God was reconciling the world to himself" (2 Cor. 5:19).

The Place of Guilt and Joy in Vertical Grief

At this point in my literary effort about God's grief and ours, I choose to make an assertion: Guilt resolution between God and the world needs to be recaptured as belonging to grief resolution. If guilt resolution is experienced without grief resolution, we may be left in the valley of grief having met a repentance requirement that passes as forgiveness. True joy comes when forgiveness is a part of grief resolution. It is true that Jesus initiated his ministry with a call to repentance, but not as a demand to enter the kingdom of

God. It was an invitation to be reclaimed to kinship in the Kingdom that he represented through faith, hope, and love. Repentance will come from and be sustained by the joy of a restored relationship. This is the message Jesus shared in parabolic form.

Fred B. Craddock, writing about the parables of Jesus in his commentary on Luke, placed the emphasis of the Christian message not on the sorrow of losing but on the joy of finding what is lost.[3] In Luke 15:3-32, the Gospel writer tells three stories about loss: a lost sheep, a lost coin, and a lost son.

In the parables about a lost sheep (vv. 3-7) and a lost coin (vv. 8-10) there is a seeking until the sheep and the coin are found. The seeker will not give up until that which is lost is found. To Jesus, this is a picture of God's relentless quest to restore to relationship those who are separated from God. He will not rest until he experiences the joy of a party of celebration of having back what was lost.

In the parable of the lost son (vv. 11-32) the father represents God, and the two sons represent humanity—all of us. The father loves both sons—the one who stays at home and the one who leaves home to dwell in a far country. There is implied in the younger son's leaving the freedom that God gives us to make life-determining decisions.

Away from the father, the son wastes his inheritance on foolish and immoral living and ends up taking a job feeding pigs. There, he comes to himself and realizes he is lost, lost from a father who loves him and from a home where he had sonship status. At this point of the story I see a son, homesick and grieving for his father and family, experiencing genuine repentance evoked from what he once had and lost. His grief over what he has lost brings him to repentance—not repentance that brings him to grief.

He leaves the far county and returns home and confesses his transgressions and asks for servant status, not restored sonship. How will the father answer his son? Will he make him a servant? Will he send him back to the foolish life he had freely chosen? No! The father ends his grief and his son's by replacing the son's rags with the clothes of restored sonship and by throwing a party of joy with music, dancing, and banquet food. His son was lost, but now is found.

That's how God celebrates when we come to ourselves and return to him from our far countries. There is homecoming joy in God's heart. That's the way God's grief ends—not in the acceptance of his loss, but in the acceptance home of his lost child.

In this story of the prodigal son, the older brother is out on the farm and asks a servant what the celebration music means. When he discovers his brother has returned and his father is throwing him a "welcome home" party, the older brother refuses to participate, telling his father, "I have worked hard for you and you never gave me a party." The father responds, "Son, you are always with me, and all that is mine is yours. Your brother was dead, and is alive; he was lost, and is found."

That's the way the parable ends, with the father demonstrating his love for both sons. Like this father, Jesus wants all of God's children to know they have a place at the Father's table. That is his main focus: the Father's celebrative love when we return home to him and to ourselves.

Is Jesus in this story of the prodigal son? I do not think it is inconsistent with the story's core meaning to see Jesus standing in for the older brother. Through the centuries in the church, the body of Christ, Jesus has been referred to as "our elder brother." In that family role he does for us what the older brother does not do. He comes into the far country—a world lost from a father's love—and says to all of us prodigals, "Greater love has no man than this, that a man lay down his life for his friends" (John 15:13). Then, as our older brother, he dies for us on a Roman cross and is God's love in human flesh, calling us to reclaim our family ties as sons and daughters being re-created in the image of God. In Jesus, our grief and God's grief end in the beginning joy of being at home in the Father's house.

Full Redemption as Both Gift and Process

Our being home in the Father's house, however, is not a finished reality. We still live in a creation that groans toward perfection (see Rom. 8:22-25). The work of God's redemption through Jesus Christ, then, is both gift and process. The gift is acceptance as sons and daughters. The process is reclaiming the meaning of the image of God revealed in Jesus Christ. He is the example and mentor in whom we see the fullness of the restored image of God.

In the four Gospels we see in human form a person whose core definition is faith, hope, love, and grace—with grace-filled love pulsating through and guiding all of the characteristics of his divine and human selfhood. As the essence of who God is, he is our redeemer. As the example of who we can be in the fullness of spiritual and relational maturity, he is our mentor.

In writing about the church as the body of Christ, Paul sees it this way: "Rather, speaking the truth in love, we are to grow up in every way into him who is the head, into Christ, from whom the whole body, joined and knit together by every joint with which it is supplied, when each part is working properly, makes bodily growth and up builds itself in love" (Eph. 4:15-16).

And, as we continue to live in the far country and the image of God becomes dim again and our spirits and the spirit of our Father grieve within us, let us come to the Lord's table (which is our Father's table) with our confession of faith, hope, love—and transgressions—and renew the joy of our salvation and our commitment to share our joy with those who still grieve in a world filled with ephemeral joys.

The closer we come to having faith, hope, and love as our core definition, the closer we will come toward being at home in the Father's house, and the closer we will come toward reclaiming the image of God revealed in Christ in all of our relationships. Here is Paul's take on this:

> From now on, therefore, we regard no one from a human point of view; even though we once regarded Christ from a human point of view, we regard him thus no longer. Therefore, if anyone is in Christ, he is a new creation; the old has passed away, behold, the new has come. All this is from God, who through Christ reconciled us to himself and gave us the ministry of reconciliation; that

is, in Christ God was reconciling the world to himself, not counting their trespasses against them, and entrusting to us the message of reconciliation. (2 Cor. 5:16-19)

In other words, God does not end his grief and ours over our broken relationship by accepting the loss. Instead, he provides a way—reconciliation through Christ—to accept back those whom he has lost.

When, therefore, guilt resolution is separated from grief resolution, repentance may become a legalistic requirement that produces an initial joy that fades under a perception that God's love is at the service of his judgment instead of judgment being at the service of his love. When guilt resolution is a part of grief resolution, repentance is not a requirement necessary to produce acceptance on God's part: it is an invitation back to our true selves as persons created by love (God) for love (God). When we are reconciled (through Christ) to that kind of joyful repentance as dynamic change toward higher levels of authentic maturity in faith, hope, and love, that is gospel! That is good news!

I have read somewhere that confession is good for the soul, so I have a confession to make: The image of God in Frank Hawkins is not a fixed and finished reality. There are days and chunks of time when love at the center of my inner concentric circle is my core definition. As I interact with others (my wife, family members, friends, and strangers), however, love becomes removed—consciously, perhaps at times unconsciously—from my center, and is replaced by other characteristics that have good purposes when they are at the service of love, but that become disintegrative and harmful when they replace love at my center.

Sometimes anger, a characteristic of God and us (as persons created in his image) replaces love. When it does, instead of being at love's service, anger becomes harmful and hateful. This is true of all of our "created in the image of God" traits—judgment, goodness, wisdom, knowledge, power, and so on. When this displacement of love happens in me, I feel a sense of loss, a feeling of sorrow that says, "You are separated from the Father's house. You are not yourself. You are separated from love and the joy that only restored love can bring." It is this grieving to be restored, this grieving of my spirit by the grieving of God's spirit, that brings me back to myself as a son of God, journeying toward a time when I will be one with God (love) and the image of God within me will be whole.

All of us are finite humans yearning for and seeking fulfillment and wholeness. We are not in this world by accident or chance. Someone—not something—brought us here with good intentions in mind. In spite of the darkness and chaos we observe around us and in us, this Someone is still at work bringing all of Creation to completion. God chooses not to complete this work alone. Through his infinite wisdom at the service of love, God chooses to work in collaboration with us to complete his creation.

Just as God works through communion and community, so must we. Just as God works through history (ours and the world's) with indestructible hope to finish what love started, so must we. We may differ in methods about how we view the task at hand, but our collaboration must be consistent with a purpose greater than private, provincial, sectarian, and national goals.

And, what is this greater purpose? Is it not the redemptive changing of lives in a communal setting where imperfect humans open their lives to God and one another, not as requirement and demand, but as invitation to God's kingdom of grace, forgiveness, and growth?

In a microcosm illustration, here's what I believe the term "kingdom of God" means universally and personally: A woman in her 20s showed up one Sunday morning for a Sunday School class meeting. She had made some unfortunate choices that had brought her much pain, anxiety, and sorrow. That morning the women of the class became a repentance-experiencing community. Risking themselves, they shared information about themselves where they wanted to grow. They were not seeking sentimental forgiveness from the class and from God. They wanted help enough to bring their hurts and areas of needed change before the judgment and forgiveness of a community of imperfect peers whom they trusted. To be sure, God was at work in that class.

The visitor said nothing. The following Sunday she returned and listened. Several class members reported progress and growth with their relational challenges. They spoke of growth in terms of being freer in their relations with God and others, especially family members. That morning, in that context where the church was experiencing repentance in an atmosphere of trust and openness, the young woman ceased to feel like an outsider. She risked herself by sharing her pain and sense of hopelessness. The class heard her without condemning her. They accepted her into their quest for growth through a process of durable attitudinal change. This occurred in the presence of God's forgiveness and judgment, incarnated by the church in a small group meeting.

The young woman had seen a practical demonstration of true repentance. In that setting, love—in quest of wholeness—had cast out her fear of change. The writer of 1 John 4 surely has it right: "In this is love perfected with us, that we may have confidence for the day of judgment, because as he is, so are we in the world. There is no fear in love, but perfect love casts out fear. For fear has to do with punishment, and he who fears is not perfected in love. We love, because he first loved us" (vv. 17-19).

True church—and true religion—is a relational place where repentance is experienced, not demanded. It is a place where imperfect, lost, and grieving people are welcomed back to a grieving and loving Father by imperfect and loving people who make room at the family table: "Blessed are those who mourn, for they shall be comforted" (Matt. 5:14). And in that comfort, our grief is transformed into joy: "These things I have spoken to you, that my joy may be in you, and that your joy may be full" (John 15:11). At the communion table, God nourishes us with his sacrificial life in Jesus Christ. Then, with renewed strength and hope, we journey on toward his eternal table of unending joy and discovery.

Notes

[1] William F. Lynch, *Images of Hope* (London: University of Notre Dame Press, 1974), 129-177.

[2] Søren Kierkegaard, *Purity of Heart* (New York: Harper and Row, 1946), 31-38.

[3] Fred B. Craddock, *Luke, Interpretation: A Biblical Commentary for Teaching and Preaching* (Louisville, KY: John Knox Press, 1990), 183-188.

Biblical Examples of Vertical Grief

In the Bible we find stories of vertical grief being resolved in the joy of restored relationships. Perhaps spending some time with Jacob, Jonah, and Zacchaeus will help us to understand better the mysterious and wonderful ways God moves to make this possible.

Longing for the Primary Blessing

All of us grow up in imperfect family systems that come from imperfect family streams. With the best of intentions, we vow to fix our system and render its future flow blessed without dysfunction. Often we succeed in making improvements, but flaws remain. In the moving stream we look to parents, grandparents, and others to bless us so we can bless our offspring and posterity. In his book, *The Power to Bless*, Myron Madden deals with this human need to bless and to be blessed.[1] This longing is as old as human civilization.

Abram, as he left his ancient home, Ur of the Chaldeans, received a divine promise: "I will bless you, and make your name great, so that you will be a blessing" (Gen. 12:2). The divine parent spoke to this human need to be blessed and to bless. Isaac, Abraham and Sarah's child of promise, received an imperfect parental blessing that he in turn sought to pass on to his children, especially Esau, his older son. According to the family customs of those ancient times, the oldest male child would receive the primary blessing from the Father. The other siblings had to divide secondary blessings. Dr. Madden, in the above cited book, makes clear that this ancient custom of blessing children is a universal and timeless process, just as active today as it was millennia ago.

How do we come to that achievement? Perhaps in spending some time with Isaac, Rebekah, Esau, and Jacob, we can better participate in this estate of affirmation and goodness for which we long, grieve, and hope.

In this ancient family story (Genesis 25-33), Rebekah and Jacob deceive Isaac and Esau so that Jacob, not Esau, receives the primary blessing. Esau becomes angry and vows to kill his blessing-grabbing brother. Rebekah, hearing Esau's threat, counsels her younger son to flee to Haran and seek refuge with her brother, Laban. Jacob leaves home with a stolen, primary blessing. The blessing, however, is flawed, not only because it is stolen, but also because it is an unrealistic expectation in human relationships. Jacob leaves home not as a possessor of the primary blessing, but as a pilgrim seeking it.

Home, family, and parents do bless; they also bestow on their children the flaws of their imperfections and sins. Jacob experiences this mixture of the positives and negatives, and will seek to banish his grief as a nagging sense that life must yield a greater fulfillment—that estate of complete blessedness. He seeks it first in marriage.

When Jacob arrives in Haran, he meets Rachel at a well where she comes to water her father's sheep. After assisting her with the sheep and giving her a kinsman's kiss, or perhaps a kiss of first love, Rachel runs home and tells her father that company has arrived. Laban welcomes Jacob to his home and allows him to work for a month with no strings attached. Then comes the offer: Laban invites Jacob to unpack his bags and work for wages. Jacob commits to work for seven years for the hand of Rachel in marriage. Laban agrees and Jacob begins his labor of love that seems very brief to him.

Completing his agreement, Jacob asks for his wages—Rachel. Laban throws a wedding party, but Jacob winds up in bed with Leah, Rachel's weak-eyed, older sister. Jacob protests the deception. All of a sudden the tables are turned: Jacob deceived his father and older brother, and now his father-in-law and his older daughter deceive Jacob. Laban cites their family tradition that the oldest daughter must be given in marriage first. Jacob agrees to work seven more years for Rachel. He now must live with two quarreling sisters. Marriage does not bring to Jacob that estate of full blessedness. That's too much to ask from Rachel or Leah—or any marriage partner

During my 52 years as a pastor I have counseled numerous couples who have come to marriage expecting their partners to make them completely happy. These marriages have moved in one of two directions. Some of them have come to terms with unrealistic expectations, and have freed their marriages from the burden of being the ultimate source of their blessedness. Other marriages have been dissolved in divorce, as one or both of the partners continue to seek someone who can give the ultimate blessing. I have seen some of these find partners in a second marriage with whom they do develop a greater mutuality. Others seem to never give up on finding a blessing that no one human is capable of giving to another.

Jacob continues to seek the blessing. He does not give up on marriage but does not limit his quest to it. He turns to vocational fulfillment. In fact, during the 14 years he works for Rachel and Leah, he is the catalyst for the remarkable success that comes to Laban's economy. Laban is aware of this and wants to keep Jacob as a junior officer in his firm. Again, he offers Jacob wages. This time Jacob is not interested; he wants the blessing of ownership. Through negotiations, based on deception between father-in-law and son-in-law, Jacob achieves his dream: the blessings of wealth and prosperity.

Now he's ready to go home and show how blessed he is. And yet, something bothers Jacob. Where is the primary blessing? He left home with it, he thought. He has been blessed with wives, children, and wealth. Something is still missing, though; he grieves for a blessing he has not experienced. With that sense of incompleteness, Jacob journeys toward home. Perhaps there is in him a belief that the blessing will come as he faces his past with its deceptiveness.

The crisis comes when he is informed that Esau and 400 of his men are coming to meet him. Will this be payback time—Esau's season of revenge? Jacob sends gifts to his brother by his servants, hoping to diminish his anger. Then he secures his family by the ford of the Jabbok as prelude to a sleepless night of wrestling with someone by the stream. Who was that someone, and why were they wrestling?

I see Jacob wrestling with one who represents the divine presence. And, of course, we can only imagine how the conversation unfolded as they wrestled.

I hear Jacob as he confesses: "All of my life I have sought the blessing, but it has eluded me. I stole my brother's birthright and blessing. It was not enough. Then I worked 14 years to possess the woman I truly love. I have been blessed by Rachel and Leah who have given me sons and daughters, but that was not enough. Then I became rich with cattle, sheep, goats, and servants. Now here I am alone, blessed but unblessed, striving with a presence whose name I do not know, but I will not let you go unless you bless me."

Then his wrestling partner asks, "What is your name?" and receives the answer, "Jacob." Then the unnamed party says, "Your name shall no more be called Jacob, but Israel, for you have striven with God and with men, and have prevailed." Then Jacob asks him, "Tell me, I pray, your name." But he responds with a question: "Why is it that you ask my name?" And there he blesses him (Gen. 32:26-29).

I truly believe that wrestling match was rigged. I'm convinced that the unnamed one wanted Jacob to win and receive the primary blessing.

So, there he goes limping toward a rising sun. He is Israel, ready to encounter and bless Esau, ready to bless with the blessing he has received. And the limp? I'm not sure what its full meaning might be. To the Jews it has ceremonial significance. To me it has relational meaning. Even when we receive the primary blessing from a God whose name we do know in Jesus Christ, we still have a limp, a longing, a grieving for a blessing that will be known as "Messiah time." Until then, "blessed are those who mourn" (Matt. 4:4).

Grieving with God

The book of Jonah is a story about a small country, Israel, told as the Jewish people try to maintain their national identity amid empire-size countries. One of the empires, Egypt, enslaved the Jews for centuries. The God of Abraham, Isaac, and Jacob delivered them and led them to a promised land, Canaan, whose possession was won through battles, defeats, sacrifices, and victories. After achieving statehood, Israel faced the humiliation of being occupied at various times by Assyria, Babylonia, Persia, Greece, and Rome.

It is no surprise, then, that when God instructs Jonah to go to Nineveh, the capital city of the Assyrian Empire, he refuses to go. Not only does he refuse to go, but he also boards a ship at Joppa and sets sail for Tarshish, a city at the other end of the Mediterranean Sea. Perhaps he thinks the trip will give God time to cool off and realize the Ninevites have their own gods.

What a foolish idea, the Jewish people must have thought. Surely God must have gotten it wrong. After all, Nineveh is the enemy. We can imagine them saying, "Let them have their destiny and we'll have ours. We don't want a present or a future destiny mixed with those who are different from us. They say you are plural. We say you are one—singular. They must be from some other source, but not you, God. We're from you, and let's just keep it that way—exclusive and pure. If we mix it up, either we'll become absorbed in them and lose our identity as your chosen ones, or they will adulterate our purity and you will cease to be singular and become just one in a plurality of choices."

Can we blame the Jewish people? They had suffered slavery, exile, and the humiliation of being occupied by enemies just like the Ninevites. Would we have joined Jonah in his flight away from God's call to go to Nineveh?

According to the story, God sends a storm that threatens to destroy the ship, its cargo, and passengers. The sailors pray to their gods for deliverance while Jonah sleeps below, knowing the storm is a message from God to him. When the sailors arouse him to pray to his God, too, Jonah confesses that he and his disobedience provoked God to send the storm, and if they throw him in the ocean, the storm will cease. At first they refuse (there is goodness in the crew who do not believe in Jonah's God). Finally they give in and cast Jonah in the sea. The storm ceases. Jonah is swallowed by a giant fish and remains there for three days. In the belly of the fish he expresses some form of repentance, but not repentance that changes his heart.

The fish finally has enough of Jonah and regurgitates him alive close to land. From there, Jonah obeys God's command and enters Nineveh with a message of God's judgment. To his surprise, the people of Nineveh, including the king, repent in sackcloth and ashes and God reveals his true purpose in Jonah's mission to Nineveh: He wants them to be included in his circle of mercy, compassion, forgiveness, and kinship. Jonah is angered and says, "I knew it! I knew you would go soft and be merciful." Then he builds a shelter east of Nineveh and waits, hoping that God's mercy will give way to judgment and the city will be destroyed.

Jonah is unaware that God is about to use his shelter to teach him, and us, a timeless lesson about all humankind. God creates a plant that immediately provides shade and protection for Jonah from the intensely hot sun. Jonah enjoys his shade. Then God sends a worm that destroys the plant. Jonah grieves over the loss of the plant and expresses a death wish over the loss of his source of comfort.

Then comes the question to Jonah and to us: "You grieve over the loss of things that bring you passing comforts—things you didn't create, that can exist one day and are gone the next. Shouldn't I grieve over people I created in my own image and are related to me through Creation, just as much as you are?"

If we still have doubts about the existence of vertical grief—God's grief over a world separated from him—denying its brotherhood and sisterhood because it grieves over lost comforts while being in danger of losing its capacity to grieve its loss of the Father of us all, let us listen again to God's question to Jonah and to his world: "Shouldn't I grieve?" And if we truly belong to this grieving God, we must answer, "Yes, you must grieve and so must we, until the anger and judgments of this world become like your anger and judgments toward Nineveh—servants of your mercy, compassion, and love."

Offering Grace to All

As we approach the end of this literary walk through the valley of grief, I want to invite you to play a child's game called "I like you, I don't like you." Parents may ask their children, "Why do you play with Jim, Bob, Jane, and Betty?" They may answer, "'Cause, we like them." "Well, why don't you play with Larry, Hazel, and Frank?" They may answer, "'Cause we don't like them." Their lists of "likes" and "don't likes" tend to be quite flexible.

For example, when Pat and I were missionaries in Brazil in the late 1960s our children, Perri, Greg, and Todd, played with their Brazilian friends just about every day. One day Greg came home crying. "I'll never play with Alfredo again," he said. He and Alfredo had gotten into a fight while playing soccer. Alfredo made the same pledge to his parents. The next day they were playmates again. Their friendship was too strong to keep each other on their "I don't like you" lists. Alfredo's dad shared with me a note his son wrote to himself and placed by his pillow. It said, "Remember, you can't play with Greg anymore." Evidently, he was afraid he might forget. He did! So did Greg.

As we leave the innocence of childhood and begin to live in a world based on competition, our "like" and "don't like" lists tend to become less flexible. Consider these questions:

- Who is on your "I don't like you" lists?
- How does God feel toward those on your lists?
- Does God have an "I don't like you" list?
- Does God have an unalterable "I favor you" list?
- Does God have an unalterable "I disfavor you" list?

The Bible gives us an answer to the question about who can receive the favor of God's grace. It is shared in story form in the Gospel of Luke (19:1-10) as Jesus is on his way to Jerusalem and makes a stop in Jericho.

Now, Jericho is no "little hick town." From numerous sources we learn of its rich and colorful history. It is associated with the earliest battles of the Jewish people to take possession of the Promised Land. It is a beautiful city, made more beautiful by Mark Anthony when he gave it to his mistress Cleopatra on the Nile River. It is a city of tragedy. When Herod the Great ruled there, he made sure there would be grief at his funeral by prearranging the slaying of some of the leading Jericho citizens to mark the occasion. It is a crowded city. Farmers, merchants, and teachers enjoy the beautiful gardens as they process their goods at Jericho's strategic location in relation to the eastern and northern caravan routes. And, temple priests and officials love to reside there, and have no problem traveling the Jericho road to perform their cultic duties in Jerusalem. Jericho is also a center of the hated Roman tax program, one that includes taxes on many items, including balsam (balm of Gilead) and the expensive imports from Damascus and the East.

Jericho is best remembered, especially among Christians, because Jesus, on his way to Jerusalem, stops there and meets a man named Zacchaeus—a man on everyone's "I don't like you" list. Politically and economically, he is considered a traitor and a thief. He is working for the Romans, their enemy, as a chief tax collector and has become rich by overcharging. Socially, if there is a party among Jericho Jews, Zacchaeus is not invited. Religiously, he is no longer considered a part of those waiting for the coming of the Messiah. What will this lost and hopeless rich man do?

He hears there is a prophet in town who welcomes even tax collectors and sinners. He wants to see if it's true. He joins the pushing and shoving crowd gathered to see the traveling evangelist. Because of the crowd, he climbs a sycamore tree (some say a kind of wild fig tree). Jesus comes to the tree and stops, spotting Zacchaeus. The crowd waits to hear Jesus' words. Will Jesus put Zacchaeus on his "I don't like you" list? That would be the religiously correct thing to do. That would put Jesus on the crowd's "I like you" list and on their perception of God's "I like you" list. Instead, Jesus sees a grieving, lonely man, rich materially but in spiritual rags, waiting to hear a word of compassion and comfort, not a word of condemnation. "Zacchaeus, make haste and come down, for I must stay at your house today" (Luke 19:5).

This day, before Jesus goes to his death near Jerusalem, the Messiah visits Jericho. In his visit, he asks for hospitality from a sinner. This is the way salvation works: It's not our repentance that releases God's grace in our lives. It is God's grace seeking an invitation into our hearts and homes that makes repentance as the power to change possible. And, like Zacchaeus, we then are inspired to accept through faith renewed sonship and daughtership at the Father's table, where Jesus is the host.

The story ends with Zacchaeus pledging to use his wealth to more than compensate those whom he has wronged, while also being generous to the poor. Then Jesus reveals a new status for Zacchaeus and his household: "Today salvation has come to this house, since he also is a son of Abraham. For the Son of man came to seek and to save the lost" (Luke 19:9-10). Not only is Zacchaeus restored to the Abrahamic community that anticipated the coming of the Messiah, but he also is given a new name and a new status by the incarnate Messiah whom he receives as a house guest. Isn't this the glad invitation we are to extend to the world: a new name and a new status?

Back in the early 1970s, Rob Sellers became a missionary Journeyman serving in Indonesia with career missionary Bill O'Brien. One day Rob and Bill were walking along a busy street in the city of Jakarta. Up ahead they saw a crowd gathered around someone who had fallen. That someone turned out to be a little girl. When an ambulance arrived to take the unconscious child to the hospital, there were no family members present to claim her. Rob and the resident missionary followed the ambulance to the hospital. Because there were no family members there to identify her, the hospital listed her as "no name."

Rob and Bill visited the little girl while she was recovering in the hospital. They became her friends, and when she was discharged (with no one to claim her as a family member), they took her to the missionary community where she received physical, emotional, and spiritual care. The day came when the little girl received Jesus as her Savior and Lord. Rob said he will never forget that day and her baptism that followed.

Standing in a nearby river, with her adoptive family supporting from the bank, Bill O'Brien said, "I baptize you my sister in the name of the Father, the Son, and the Holy Spirit." Rob said in that moment a revelation gripped the entire group: In Christian baptism, those who have no name receive a new name and a new status as brothers and sisters and sons and daughters of our eternal Father. And, at our baptism the words that were spoken at Jesus' baptism, "This is my beloved Son, with whom I am well pleased" (Matt. 3:17), continue to be spoken by our Father who claims us, redeems us, and nourishes us through his Son. And his Father's grief and ours is transformed into family joy at his table of grace, acceptance, and forgiveness.

After his sojourn in Indonesia, Rob Sellers became the minister of youth at St. John's Baptist Church in Charlotte, North Carolina. While there, he co-authored a youth musical based on the story of the little girl in Indonesia who was adopted and given a new name. He called it *The Name Givers*. What a privilege! What a gift! What a joy! What a table!

Note

[1] Myron Madden, *The Power to Bless* (Nashville: Abingdon Press, 1970), 15-60.

EPILOGUE

The Various Faces of Tears

Join me now at our Lord's table as we finish this book. That puts all of us on the same level. Here at the family table I want to ask you a question: When was the last time you can remember crying? Was it last week? Was it last month or last year? You may say, "Oh, but I don't cry." But you do. Someone has said there are dry tears or silent tears. You may not shed them on your face, but you do shed them on the inside.

We all cry. Our creator has given us the biological equipment for crying. All of us have tear ducts and tear canals. If you look closely, you can see the little openings through which the tears flow.

Have you ever noticed how people cry for different reasons? Whatever those reasons are, I believe our Lord welcomes our tears at the family table. The day will come, according to Revelation, when he will return and wipe our tears away. For now, however, we cry and our tears have meaning. Let's look, then, at the various faces of tears.

Some people cry when they experience joy. I have seen tears of joy at weddings. Sometimes when I look at the mother of the bride she is crying. Then when I ask, "Who gives this woman to be married to this man?" the father of the bride will answer, "Her mother and I," and the tears will come. They are tears of joy. He's not joyful about getting rid of his daughter; he is happy because of parental love being fulfilled in marital love. There is a significant place for the tears of joy at our Father's table.

There are people who cry when they laugh. If you knew the family of my birth, you would know persons who, when they laugh heartily, start crying. I don't know how God has put you together biologically and emotionally, but that's the way my family does it—especially my mother and Aunt Sally.

Back in the 1980s, when we were living in Kingsport, Tennessee, we had a family picture board in our kitchen. In the middle of it was a picture of Pat and me as we were leaving for our honeymoon. Placed all around that picture were photos of family members, friends, and shared happenings. When I saw the images of my mother and Aunt Sally, I remembered how they used to laugh.

Some people, when they laugh, laugh in the nose area. Others laugh in the eyes, the nose, and the mouth. But there are people who laugh all over. Mom and Aunt Sally laughed all over. Their toes got into their laughter. Then, at a certain point in their laughing, tears would begin to flow down their faces. That's the way life put them together. There is a place for the gift of laughter at the family table. Sometimes it gives us blessed release from stress and burdens.

Our tears can also express a sense of wonder. I like to go out and look at the things of nature—the majestic mountains of East Tennessee, the vastness of the ocean at Wrightsville Beach in North Carolina, and the colorful changing of the seasons. When I do this, often I get lost in a sense of wonder and find myself with tears in my eyes before I know it. I'm not ashamed of that.

The most moving experience of wonder, however, did not come from the beauty of nature. It came as I stood at a hospital door looking at a young mother and her first baby. I'll never forget the expression on Joan's face and the tears in her eyes as she said, "Pastor, it's wonderful." There is a place for that kind of wonder at the family table.

There are tears that communicate the presence of pain. None of us are immune to the problem of pain. When we are truly sensitive to our fellow human beings, we will care about their sufferings. Some people perform their jobs accompanied by varying degrees of pain. Others experience pain in their intimate relationships. Some are heroes and heroines of pain. They hurt, cry, and grow spiritually in spite of it.

One form of pain is human disappointment. When my brother, Virgil, was a child, the Depression of the 1930s was full blown. One summer day somebody brought him a beautiful, luscious peach. It was his very own! Virgil ran to the community building where the men gathered to play dominoes. He walked in with the peach in his hand. Henry Jones saw the peach, reached out and grabbed it, and said, "Virgil, let me have some of that." Then he got his pocketknife and cut the peach in half and pretended to start eating it. When he looked at Virgil, he saw that tears were rolling down his face and his mouth was quivering with disappointment. Henry said that if he could have gone out and bought a bushel of peaches for Virgil Hawkins, he would have done it. Then he returned the peach to Virgil.

Children do have disappointments. Sometimes as adults we forget how they can hurt, oftentimes without revealing their feelings, but God knows about those hurts. He knows every tear that falls on the inside or outside.

Some people become anxious and tearful about growing older. For example, at a pastoral care conference I attended in Louisville, Kentucky in the spring of 1984, Dr. Myron Madden shared with us that a lady came to him for counseling and said, "Dr. Madden, I've just turned 40 and I can't stop crying. What am I going to do?" He smiled at her and said, "Just think about how it's going to be when you turn 50. When you turn 50, you'll remember how nice it was when you turned 40." She left Dr. Madden feeling happy about being 40; her tears, however, were OK.

Finally, there are tears of appreciation. I remember a lady at the First Baptist Church in Statesboro, Georgia, who shared her appreciation in a unique manner. When my family and I prepared to leave there in 1980, after serving as pastor for five years, we had the usual farewell rituals. People say things at those times that are not shared as frequently in the course of ongoing relationships.

During a reception this lady came up and grabbed my hand. There were tears in her eyes. Pat and I had moved with her family through some deep waters of hurt and pain. She didn't say a single word; she just gripped my hand, and her face said it all. I'll never forget that communication of gratitude and appreciation.

We come to this table with our tears of gratitude for what the Lord has meant to us. I remember the episode in the Bible when Jesus went to the home of Simon the Pharisee (Luke 7:36-50). Luke says it was mealtime and that a woman came in, approached the table, and began to cry. Her tears were an expression of gratitude and love. She bathed the Master's feet with her tears and wiped them away with her hair. Simon became annoyed with the woman and registered his complaint to Jesus.

Jesus responded: "Simon, two people owed a creditor—one about $50 and the other one about $1,000. Then the creditor came in and said, 'I'm going to forgive both of you.'" Jesus asked, "Who do you think was the most grateful?" Simon answered, "The one who was forgiven the most." Jesus said, "Now you've got it, Simon. This woman was forgiven a lot, and her gratitude and love are great."

When we really get in touch with what Jesus has done for us in forgiveness, we, too, gather at the table in gratitude.

Project with me now from this table to the time when Jesus Christ will return. Revelation 21:4 tells us that when he comes he will wipe away all of our tears. Well, I want to make a confession to you. When the Lord returns, I know Frank Hawkins well enough to know what I'll do. I'm going to have myself a good cry—a cry of gratitude for all he has done for me. Then I'll say, "OK, Master, wipe them away. I won't need them anymore." There will be no more crying, no more pain, no more death. Then he will take us into the eternal banquet and serve us and let us serve one another around his blessed table.

Here then is the Lord's invitation to you: Bring your tears, your emotions, everything you are on the inside, knowing that he accepts them and offers forgiveness for what needs to be forgiven, and affirms the good that is growing in you.

Isn't this what it means to be family with him at his table?

www.ingramcontent.com/pod-product-compliance
Lightning Source LLC
Chambersburg PA
CBHW071011160426
43193CB00012B/2007